DENNIS MCCANN
TAKES YOU FOR A RIDE

STORIES FROM THE BYWAYS OF IOWA, MINNESOTA, WISCONSIN, MICHIGAN AND ILLINOIS

Amherst Press
a division of Palmer Publications, Inc.
Amherst, Wisconsin

First edition
First printing

Amherst Press
A Division of Palmer Publications, Inc.
318 North Main Street
P.O. Box 296
Amherst, WI 54406

Printed in the United States of America by
Palmer Publications, Inc.
318 North Main Street
P.O. Box 296
Amherst, WI 54406

Layout and design by Amherst Press
Marketed by Amherst Press

Library of Congress Cataloging-in-Publication Data
McCann, Dennis 1950-
    Dennis McCann Takes You For a Ride/by Dennis McCann
    1st ed. p.cm. Includes bibliographical references and index.
    ISBN:0-942495-67-5

    1.Wisconsin—Description and travel Anecdotes.
    2.Wisconsin—History, Local Anecdotes.
    3.Wisconsin—Biography Anecdotes.
    4.Middle West—Description and travel Anecdotes.
    5.Middle West—History, Local Anecdotes.
    6.Middle West—Biography Anecdotes.
    7.McCann,Dennis, 1950—Journeys—Wisconsin Anecdotes.
    8.McCann,Dennis, 1950—Journeys—Middle West Anecdotes.
    9.Automobile travel—Wisconsin Anecdotes.
    10.Automobile travel—Middle West Anecdotes.I.Title.
      F586.2 .M38 1999
    917.704'33—dc21
    99-27608 CIP

DEDICATION

To my parents, for all those Sunday rides.

Dennis McCann

CONTENTS

ACKNOWLEDGMENTS

I would like to thank my bosses at Milwaukee Journal Sentinel, *especially editor Marty Kaiser,*
for granting the use of a few past columns. Thanks, as well, to Rosemary Jensen and her able staff
in the News Information Center for their generous assistance in helping locate many of the photographs
in the book. And, of course, thanks to the folks at Amherst Press for agreeing to make this collection
available to armchair travelers and Sunday drivers alike.

Most of all, thanks to all the readers who through the years have called or written to tell me where to go.
I couldn't have done it without you.

And thank you to Barbara, as always, for everything.

INTRODUCTION

TIMING IS EVERYTHING. I was lucky enough to grow up in the dying days of the Sunday ride, before color TV stole our minds, before professional football became religion, before energy shortages, computers and home entertainment centers changed all the rules.

When I was a kid in the 1950s, our entertainment center was outdoors. On Sunday we would squeeze our family of 10 (no mean trick, that) into the old station wagon to head for exotic ports of call in our little corner of Rock County, in southern Wisconsin.

We'd leave Janesville for Footville or Lima Center or Indianford or sometimes, if the sun was warm, to Shopiere to jump off the dam. We never went very far, but we always went somewhere.

Does anyone say "Hey, let's go for a ride!" today? I'll bet far less than "Hey, let's go to McDonalds."

Later I was lucky again. The *Milwaukee Journal* saved me from a life of covering meetings and politics when it hired me and told me to get lost—and then write back with what I found.

Imagine. My beat became the long and winding road. My job was, and still is, to take rides on workdays and share what I find with readers. Over the years, and over hundreds of thousands of miles, I've visited London and Rome, Berlin and Belgium, Brussels and Scandinavia and Holland, the capitals of Europe to some but exotic dots on the midwestern map to me. I've been in towns so small they use first names only, like Earl and Edgar. I found Bliss and Paradise in Michigan, roamed Minnesota from A (Austin) to Z (Zumbrota) and if you ask me about that night in Marquette I'll have to ask you to get specific. Wisconsin? Michigan? Iowa? I've been to them all.

As for what I have in common with Papa Hemingway, it's time in Key West. Of course, mine was in Iowa.

Through such travels have emerged the stories in this book. A number of them have appeared as columns in The *Milwaukee Journal* and, more recently, the *Milwaukee Journal Sentinel,* while others are appearing here for the first time. Where necessary to update columns previously published I've included explanatory postscripts. And where it might be helpful to readers who want to follow my steps in person instead of just in print, I've included destination tips.

Either way, enjoy the ride.

1
WALKING IN CIRCLES

GENEVA LAKE, WISCONSIN

AT 11 O'CLOCK ON A JUNE MORNING SO SPLENDID I could almost forgive this state for March, I followed the water's edge into Fontana, if no longer stepping lively at least still stepping right along.

Good, then. Fontana was the halfway point on the walking path that rings this playground lake, and it was here I had planned to take my pulse.

If I felt sound, I would continue on and close the circle. If key parts ached or complained, I would about-face and go back.

Kidding, of course. Even I can do that math. And the real do-or-die part of this day's walk had come three hours earlier, on the first step onto the path behind the library in Lake Geneva.

I had talked for years of walking the path that rings Geneva Lake and it was finally time to put up or shut up. So long before Fontana, no matter how loud my poor dogs were

howling, there would be no turning back.

Anyway, not a whimper. I pressed on.

Geneva is one of Wisconsin's most splendid lakes, a canvas of blue water and white sails and all the rich and subtle shades of nature's palette. The rich, mostly barons of industry and commerce from Illinois, discovered it years ago and bought up the land around Geneva for palatial summer homes and sprawling estates. Most of the original families are gone now, but in many ways this is still Chicago's toniest suburb, governed by stern "Members Only" and "Private Property" signs and home to more of those infernal and noisy "personal watercraft" than even hell will have.

Still, if the wealthy own the land around this lake, the public owns the path at water's edge. By state law, the shore path is open to the public, every step of the almost 21 miles where water meets land. It offers up-close views of mansions and landscaped lawns (often the path runs right across those lawns) and provides a name-dropping (Wrigley, Swift, Maytag, Wacker) explanation of Lake Geneva's past.

In short, it is a workaday window-peeker's paradise. This was the path I was walking on that fine June day.

I began at the Lake Geneva Public Library, carrying water for my thirst, sunscreen for my poor Irish hide, Vaseline for my toes and bagels for the soul. I carried a notebook and a pen and a good cigar to fire up in honor of Chief Big Foot, whose statue now stands in Fontana and who loved this lake long before the wealthy

arrived.

Oh, and a copy of *Walk, Talk & Gawk,* the map and guide to the shore path developed by three teachers. It offers both guidance and gossip, informing the walker that it is 3.5 miles from the library to Chapin Road, for example, as well as the fact that on the porch of the large, white mansion with blue-carpeted steps the old "Amos and Andy" show used to be broadcast in summers.

It was like that all the way, a sort of architectural and historical summer school, tuition-free to boot. Early on I passed through Green Gables, the original Wrigley estate, and marveled at mansions with names like Fair Field, Wychwood, Bonnie Brae, Glen Fern and Glen Annie, the house with the blue steps.

The path covers every type of terrain imaginable, dirt in spots, boardwalks and paving stone, concrete, long stretches of grass and in a few places narrow, steep and eroded banks. It is not a walk in the park, but the reasonably fit and adequately trained hiker should be up to what the guide suggests is an eight- or nine-hour effort.

But the lake doesn't have to be circled in one day, and here the guide is most helpful. On this weekday I met only one other man who was obviously walking the entire lake but also met a number of people out for morning constitutionals on the shore path.

Walk, Talk and Gawk cuts the hike into seven segments ranging from 2 to 3.5 miles. You could, for example, cover the 3.5 miles from Williams Bay to Fontana one day and return later to do the next leg, and the next and next. Each map offers parking tips, distances and a brief description of the land to be covered. To avoid backtracking, walking companions could use two cars and cover the lake relay-style over whatever period is desired.

You could also walk from Lake Geneva to Williams Bay and return on a Geneva Lake cruise boat.

Or, you can do-or-die it and find real accomplishment. My feet were barking a bit by the time I reached Buttons Bay, where the final leg of the walk begins at Big Foot Beach State Park. I skirted the front of the park, found the path again at the edge of town, passed by the fabulously ostentatious Stone Manor—the largest home on the lake—and finally reached downtown.

I waved to the statue of Andy Gump, whose creator had lived on the lake, and just after the Riviera Ballroom walked onto the sand beach behind the library, where 6 hours and 28 minutes after I set out I removed my shoes and socks and waded knee-deep in the water.

And where, just before I struck my "Rocky" pose, I set my tender foot upon a rock. Man, did that dog howl!

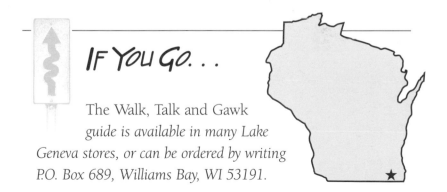

IF YOU GO. . .

The Walk, Talk and Gawk *guide is available in many Lake Geneva stores, or can be ordered by writing* P.O. Box 689, Williams Bay, WI 53191.

2
UP THE DOWN BLUFF

DUBUQUE, IOWA

THERE IS A MOMENT—ALMOST AS LONG AS THE RIDE, actually—when you think that gravity must prevail. Halfway up the bluff, that is steeper than Wisconsin taxes, the first-time rider looks back and decides it is hopeless, that the little boxcar with its frail human cargo must creak to a stop, then hurtle down the slope and crash into smithereens at the foot of Fenelon Place.

It has to. Doesn't it? What goes up, up, up must....

But it hasn't done that in a century, not since the days when the little car was secured by vulnerable ropes instead of steel cables, and before worry can even approach panic the ride is over and you are deposited on top of the world, or at least on the top of Iowa, with a view that stretches into Wisconsin and Illinois across the great river that defines this place. Not bad for 75 cents. A nap would be the historically proper gesture but who could close his eyes to such magnificent views?

J. K. Graves could. This was a man who had to have his sleep.

To appreciate the shortest, steepest railway in the world, as the 296-foot-long Fenelon Place Elevator Company claims to be, it helps to understand the geography of Dubuque. The city is built on seven hills, like Rome according to the locals. The downtown business district grew up on the flatland at the base of the hills, while many grand residences were sprinkled across the top to take advantage of the view.

One who lived atop the hill was Graves, a former mayor, promoter of mining and a banker in the 1880s, when it was customary to close downtown businesses for 90 minutes at midday and go home to dinner.

That caused problems for Graves, not to mention for his poor carriage horse. His bank was only two-and-a-half blocks from his house, but it took Graves more than 30 minutes to ride around the bluff and 30 more to ride back. That left time for lunch, but not for the nap he wanted as dessert.

So in 1882 Graves won a franchise from the city to construct a cable car similar to those he had seen climbing the steep hills of Europe. His car, modeled after those in the Alps, was powered by a coal-fired steam boiler and winch and was pulled up and down on two rails by a hemp rope. After it went into operation on July 25, 1882, Graves was raised and lowered by his gardener and was presumably much better rested for his investment.

Any homeowner who ever had a pickup truck knows what happened next. Neighbors began showing up asking for rides. So two years later, after his first elevator burned, Graves built another one with passengers in mind and began

charging five cents a ride.

In 1893 the elevator suffered another fire. Because of a poor economy Graves could not afford to build another cable car but his neighbors, by then dependent upon the elevator to get to work and other appointments, formed the Fenelon Place Elevator Company and began shopping for a better system. They settled on a cable car pulled by steel cables this time, since each time fire had come in contact with the hemp rope, fire had prevailed and the little car had indeed crashed down the bluff.

By 1912 C. B. Trewin had assumed sole ownership. The automobile—and the unfortunate end of the custom of taking noontime naps—eliminated much of the elevator's role but it was spared obsolescence when visitors to Dubuque discovered the fun. It is still operated today by Trewin's descendants, chugging up and down the bluff with tourists in tow.

"My last workday this year I get to take Mr. and Mrs. Santa down," said Bruce Oeschger, who grew up riding the cable car to deliver his newspaper route on the top of the hill and has worked as cable car operator for nine seasons. "That's kind of the official start of the shopping season in Dubuque."

On the busiest days of summer the cable car might carry 600 or more visitors up the bluff. Sometimes when paddle wheel boats pause in Dubuque passengers will be brought over to shop in the stores at the foot of the elevator and ride up and down the bluff. Not many locals use it these days, though one woman who had lived in Dubuque for 70 years took her first ride just before I did.

"Probably 90 percent at least (are tourists)," said Amy Schadle, Trewin's great-granddaughter, who oversees the operation for her mother, the current owner. "Everybody hops in their car and goes out west these days. Once they built the mall, you know how people are, everybody gets in the car and goes."

I don't understand anyone who would take the mall over the Mississippi, but that may explain why I rode the bluff alone. Once in the evening to see the lights, again in the morning to see the sights.

And in between, now that I think about it, I slept. Somewhere, J. K. Graves must have approved.

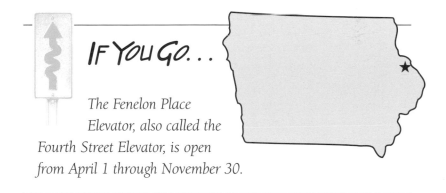

If You Go. . .

The Fenelon Place Elevator, also called the Fourth Street Elevator, is open from April 1 through November 30.

3
HISTORIC HOTEL SPARKLES AGAIN

MARQUETTE, MICHIGAN

SURPRISES COME IN ONLY TWO FORMS ON THE ROAD, pleasant and decidedly otherwise, and the sour sort lead in the standings. Or maybe they just stay with you longer, the way a scar outlasts a smile every time.

But there can be unexpected delights.

Years ago, the old Hotel Northland was one of the premier resting places in the Upper Peninsula, serving everyone from visiting business travelers to the big names of Hollywood. But as time wore on, the old hotel on the hill overlooking Lake Superior wasn't making pleasant memories. Its appearance turned dowdy, business fell off and the full-service hotel became an increasingly seedy rooming house.

Eventually, said the *Marquette Mining Journal,* the hotel that had once housed stars from Amelia Earhart to Bud Abbott and Lou Costello became "a squalid, vacant blemish on the city's skyline."

I knew nothing about that the day I needed a room in Marquette, noticed a one-inch ad in a travel guide for the Landmark Inn and made a reservation. In fact, I was almost in Marquette before I realized I hadn't even asked if I would have a private bath. So imagine my surprise to be greeted by a valet parking attendant, to find a room not only with whirlpool bath but plush bathrobes as well and, after a wonderful dinner in the hotel dining room, to discover cheesecake on the bedside table, delivered by the turn-down staff while I was gone.

Oh yes, the fireplace was lit.

Toto, we're not in the Upper Peninsula any more. The old Northland hadn't moved an inch from its place on the hill, but it had come a long, long way.

Every traveler should be so surprised.

It took more than a name change for the Northland to find new life as Landmark Inn, of course. It took sweat, almost $5 million and the dedication of owners willing to gamble everything on a building's rebirth, an especially tricky proposition at a time when a nearby military base was closing and some feared for the city's future.

In fact, the current owners bought the gutted building from another developer who had begun to restore the hotel but then gave up.

"Worried?" said Christine Pesola, who with her husband, Bruce, undertook the restoration in 1995.

"No," she said, and then grinned. "But we weren't thinking. Maybe it's better not knowing. It's total naiveté, really, but maybe that's how it works."

But they weren't totally naive, because the onetime blemish is now a jewel, an elegant hotel all the nicer for its deep bow to Marquette's rich history. There are 62 guest rooms, ranging from standard rooms with two beds to suites with fireplaces, and every suite is different from the rest, each one named for a locally significant historical figure and decorated in appropriate style.

My room was the Amelia Earhart, named for the famous flier who once landed in Marquette. The Dandelion Cottage Room was named for the subject of a regionally-known children's book by Carroll Watson Rankin in 1904. The Charlie Kawbawgam suite, with its handmade four-poster bed and furniture of birch, remembers a Chippewa Indian who lived near Marquette, and even Theodore Roosevelt has a suite in his honor, complete with photo of him speaking to a crowd in Marquette.

The suite named for George Shiras has the noted wildlife photographer's pictures on the wall and his old steamer trunk as part of the furniture. And anyone who has ever read, or seen, "Anatomy of a Murder" or any of local writer John Voelker's works (his pen name was Robert Traver) would want to ask for the Voelker suite.

The cast of the movie—Jimmy Stewart, Lee Remick, George C. Scott among them—stayed at the old Northland during filming of the movie in the 1950s. A Michigan Supreme Court judge before he resigned to write full-time, Voelker was a frequent patron in the popular bar on the top of the old Northland, a comfortable room with a terrific harbor view that was also included in the new Landmark.

Local historian Ben Mukkala produced biographies of those whose names grace the suites, so the uninformed guest will leave not merely rested but more knowledgeable, too.

Because they were granted historic preservation tax credits the Pesolas were required to spend extra for certain historic details, but Christine Pesola said the project had benefited from it.

The lobby, for example, has the rich look of the original

hotel, right down to the "historically correct paneling."

And despite Marquette's famous long winters and distance from population centers, she is confident the hotel will be a draw in itself. Skiers and snowmobilers will especially enjoy the sauna and whirlpools in the recreation area.

"I feel confident that once we get someone in here, they will come back," Pesola said. "It's one of the things that's going to make Marquette a delightful place to stay."

IF YOU GO...

For information, phone the Landmark Inn at (906) 228-2580, or (888) 752-6362

4
A BRIDGE OF WOOD AND HEART

SAXEVILLE, WISCONSIN

IT WAS A BIG IDEA BORN OF NO SMALL COINCIDENCE, this beautiful wooden bridge that spans from here to way back when. Someday when they make the movie—"The Bridge of Waushara County," of course—it will include a host of rigid bureaucrats, small-town volunteers with hammers and vision, and a couple who only wanted to give back with a park filled with flowers and quiet.

I don't see a role for Clint Eastwood. But if Meryl Streep wants in, I'm sure there'd be a part.

In 1989 the Springwater Town Board was wrestling with replacement of a little bridge over the Pine River. Government bridge builders envisioned—what else?—concrete and steel and estimated it would cost $100,000. That was when board member Garth Towne found himself in Pennsylvania for a daughter's wedding, and further found himself intrigued by the area's many covered wooden bridges, one in particular.

"Lo and behold, on it there was a plaque," said Springwater resident Kermit Jorgensen, whose property begins at one end of the bridge. "It said 'Designed and built by Ithiel Towne,'" who was, in fact, a distant relative of Garth Towne.

"(Garth) came back and said, 'Boys, I know what we've got to do. We've got to have a covered bridge.'"

Well, nothing is that easy. Covered bridge? supervisors wondered. But the idea simmered and the board eventually traveled to the Chequamegon National Forest to inspect the new Smith Rapids Covered Bridge, built in a style patented by Ithiel Towne in 1820, back when he could "build his bridge by the mile and sell it by the yard." The design was simple but also strong and beautiful, and the Springwater Town Board decided to build one of its own.

Federal and state bridge builders, of course, wanted nothing to do with it. The feds wanted a two-lane structure the wooden design wouldn't accommodate (covered bridges are usually one-way) and before all the dickering and discussing was over, the cost of a concrete and steel span was up to $135,000. So the town gulped hard, told the government to keep its money and voted to build its own bridge. Wooden, of course, and covered.

The town set up a "Covered Bridge Fund" at a Wild Rose bank and an anonymous donor gave T-shirts to sell. In 1996 the old bridge was removed and concrete footings and truss construction began. Great timbers of Douglas fir, from trees up to 150 years old, were hauled in from Oregon, where they had been cut on the last steam-powered sawmill still in use in the U.S.

Trusses were constructed in a building on the farm of one of the board members, hauled to the site and swung into place by a crane—donated, of course. Rafters were bolted and roof set in place before winter. Construction resumed the next spring and lasted for several months, but there was no hurry.

"You're talking about donated labor," said Jorgensen, "and most of them were elderly men. The youngest was 54 and the oldest 87. He turned 88 before it was finished, but he was a good man. He wasn't afraid to pick up one of those big timbers and carry his end."

Meanwhile Jorgensen and his wife, Shirley, were turning

the land on their side of the bridge into a peaceful little park. They bought a gazebo and picnic tables, had a landscaper handle bushes and flowers and added concrete walkways, turning what had been the barnyard of the farm where Jorgensen grew up into a tiny eden on the banks of the Pine.

In part, he said, the park would be a tribute to George and Carrie Rasmussen, who took him and his brother in as children when they had nowhere else to go, but also a place where strangers could "enjoy the tranquility of the park setting, the plants, the sound of the water and the birds," as the guest book puts it. "Feel God's presence and enjoy your time spent here."

Covered Bridge Park was ready by June when town officials and residents hauled lawn chairs to the site and formally dedicated the "Springwater Volunteer Bridge," completed for less than $50,000, by the way, and now both are drawing strangers to Saxeville. Some come in the evening and sit in the gazebo as darkness descends, not saying much but just listening, thinking, enjoying. Visitors from five countries and more than half the state visited in the first year, a handful of weddings have taken place and daily traffic on little 24th Lane has jumped from maybe 30 cars to 50.

"They see that sign up there—Covered Bridge Road—and think, well, there must be a covered bridge," Jorgensen said.

"Then they back up. I'm expecting to hear a crash one of these days."

It would be unfortunate to mar the peace and quiet with a car crash on the highway, though I suppose it would take care of one nagging detail.

Meryl Streep as the nurse? I like it.

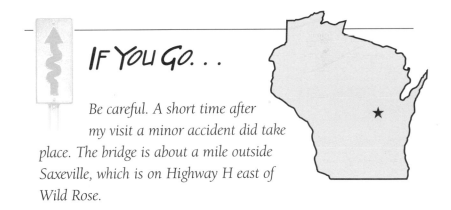

IF YOU GO. . .

Be careful. A short time after my visit a minor accident did take place. The bridge is about a mile outside Saxeville, which is on Highway H east of Wild Rose.

5
GRANT'S GALENA

GALENA, ILLINOIS

SPEND A DAY IN HISTORIC GALENA and suddenly the old "Who's buried in Grant's tomb?" doesn't seem so silly a question.

It must be someone else because the old cigar-smoking whisky sipper is alive and well in his old hometown. There's Ulysses Grant greeting buses filled with school kids and blue-haired shoppers. There's Grant stepping into the famed DeSoto House for evening refreshment, and there's the general again speaking to Civil War buffs and turning heads—oh, how he turns the heads of the unsuspecting—at his workshop on Main Street.

And there's Julia Dent Grant as well, for 37 years his beloved wife and helpmate.

Lyss, she called him in the bloodiest days of this county's history, and Lyss is what she calls him yet today. In a one-day visit to Jo Daviess County I ran into Grant at his store and met with Mrs. Grant in her home in rural Stockton and if I'd had

another day I could have shared some tea and tarts with the general's lady, if not a toddy with the man himself.

Historical hallucinations, you say. Not really. W. Paul LeGreco is General Ulysses S. Grant and Lucy Miele is Julia Dent Grant, reenacting the lives of the two most famous residents of Galena on a stage that never goes dark.

"It's the old town itself," said LeGreco, describing why the Grants and Galena are still a team after all these years. "It hasn't changed since he left. It's the old town joke. 'Don't do nothing 'til I get back.' Those were his last words."

So old red-bricked Galena looks today like it did when Grant last saw it. Why shouldn't visitors see Grant himself, stogie securely stuffed in cheek, walking its historic streets?

Oddly enough, the original Grants didn't live in Galena all that long. After his celebrated business failures in Missouri, Grant moved to Galena in 1860 to work in his father's hardware and leather store, but a year later the war required his presence. When he returned as a hero in August 1865 he and his family were presented with a fine home, but again he left after a short stay. The home, now restored and furnished in post-Civil War style, was given to the city of Galena by Grant's children in 1904.

LeGreco became Grant long before he came to Galena. Blessed with physical resemblance to the general, LeGreco won the job of playing Grant for the bicentennial exhibit at the Henry Ford Museum in Michigan in 1976. Already a collector and maker of toy soldiers, he quickly decided that an association with a hero soldier could only be good for business. The Illinois Tourism Bureau also saw opportunity and hired LeGreco to portray Grant and promote historic sites.

In 1983 that job took LeGreco-as-Grant for the first time to Galena, where he said people were so surprised to see him they followed him down the street.

Why not? They'd been awaiting his return for more than 100 years. LeGreco soon moved his toy soldier business to Galena where, dressed every day of the year as his military alter ego, he could combine his career and his pastime.

"It all came together," he said, "and I was able to recognize it at the time. I've got it all going for me."

Lucy Miele, who moved to Galena from Chicago, fell in love with the general when she began reading history. Galena sent nine generals off to civil conflict but Grant's story, the improbable redemption of a failed businessman who won the biggest war of all, was the most compelling.

"I became a great Grant enthusiast," she said. "And the more I fell in love with the general the more I fig-

Galena, Illinois

ured I better make it legal. So I married him."

And thus Julia was reborn. Miele began giving tours and telling stories and when she made her first $50 for portraying the general's lady she immediately took it down the street and bought a two-volume Grant's memoirs to learn more. Today she also portrays Dolley Madison for paying audiences but her "Tea and Tarts With the General's Lady," performed several times each summer in Galena, is her speciality.

In the one-woman show Miele tells stories about Julia Grant, explains her contribution to the general's success and, she said, walks on stage wearing every costume she will need. "I do what is an exceptionally tasteful historical striptease. If there's any little old man who's been sleeping up to that point we wake him up."

For reasons that parallel real-life the Grants work best separately. "We've only performed together once and that's when they threw a lot of money at us," LeGreco said. "She has a different style and she would completely overshadow me, as did Julia. I wouldn't be able to tell a proper story with Lucy because I would just shut up and accede to her, as he did to Julia."

So they greet separate buses, meet separate audiences. But that doesn't mean LeGreco doesn't appreciate Miele's act.

"She's my second-best advertising," he said, referring to his toy soldier store.

"I'm my best."

And then he laughed. After all these years, the general has a thriving business.

IF YOU GO. . .

Galena is in northwest Illinois, near the border of Iowa and Wisconsin. For information on attractions and accomodations for Galena and Jo Daviess County call (888) 442-5362. The number for the U.S. Grant Home State Historic Site is (815) 777-0248.

6
ISLE OF HAPPY DAYS

MIKANA, WISCONSIN

ON A SUN-BAKED PIER ON A QUIET LITTLE ISLAND in gorgeous Red Cedar Lake, two men in swimsuits and sunglasses met, chatted and exchanged stories.

You know mine. I came to write about Stout's Lodge, which meant one short night of stress-free respite and then gone on the morning pontoon.

His story was worlds better. He worked in St. Paul but owned a cottage on this island in Barron County where his family comes to spend the long, lazy days of summer. For most people, that would mean endlessly dreary commutes or weeknights alone in the city while his family frolicked.

Not for him. He had a float plane tied to another pier in a cove nearby and commuted by air— 20 miles to the little lake outside his office in the cities, 20 minutes back to the sun-baked pier on a little island and, when the sun has ended its own commute, dinner with his family in the lodge or a cook-out on the lawn.

Next year, when he turns 50, he may host a Great Gatsby gala.

It left me with two thoughts, only one of them mean, green envy.

F. D. Stout would understand this guy, I thought. The Isle of Happy Days, indeed.

Frank Stout was one of those early industrial barons who had more money than they knew what to do with, but that didn't keep them from trying. Stout was a director of the Chicago, St. Paul and Omaha Railroad who purchased half-interest in the small island a century ago to build a hunting shack and, later, a log home.

Roads then were difficult and dusty, however, so he ordered a rail line constructed so he could more easily reach his land. By 1903 Stout owned the entire island and would come with his wife, five children, nursemaids and butlers to while away the summer. They would picnic and pick blue-

insects made themselves at home, so Stout decided to rebuild. He sent a train to Idaho for perfect-as-possible cedar logs and brought in a big crew of carpenters, who were ordered to handle the logs only in snow so that no dust could scar them and to use ropes on the California redwood beams instead of chains for the same reason.

Stout envisioned a lodge styled after palatial retreats in the Adirondacks, and that's what he got. The floors were four-inch planks, the big fireplace was of carved gray stone from Italy and other materials came from Germany. There were buildings for cooks and servants, separate cabins for the children, a fine log boathouse, schoolhouse and an elaborate bell tower, still standing.

There was a billiards room and bowling alley, and when Stout decided he wanted a golf course nearby that would resemble the famed St. Andrews he imported grass seed and

berries. One of the local handymen would put the children in a clothes basket in a wheelbarrow and push them all around.

A local history called *Around the Four Corners* said it didn't take Stout long to figure out he had planned poorly when he used bark-covered logs for his buildings. Worms and a grounds crew from Scotland to build what became Tagalong Golf Course. It is said he spent $1.5 million—in 1915 dollars—and when it was done an iron plate was set on the doorstep proclaiming Stout's lodge "The Isle of Happy Days."

The Stouts are long gone, but when you step across that plate to go to your room or to enjoy dinner in the evening, it is hard to quarrel with the century-old boast. Today Stout's retreat is a public lodge offering 31 guest rooms, ranging from doubles with shared baths to separate cabins with full amenities. It still offers everything from billiards and croquet to boats and bowling but more than that it offers a quiet place on a pretty lake where the speed limit is not-so-fast, friend. What's the hurry?

"If you're a highly-stressed person," said gardener Kelly McRaith, "this is a good place to be, because it's usually quiet."

Not always. The weekend before my one-night visit, a wedding party had rented the entire island (except for the handful of privately-owned cottages). Stout's Lodge is popular for conferences and weddings but quiet is the principal commodity. In addition to the main island, a wood-and-steel bridge connects to an adjoining, undeveloped island that is a bird sanctuary, complete with bald eagle's nest.

A pontoon makes almost hourly runs for guests during the busy season, and also takes golfers to Tagalong. In addition to canoes, kayaks and paddleboats, there is also a party pontoon for big events. But simply resting is allowed as well. After a tour of the buildings and grounds, co-owner Bernie Fredrickson sent me off to relax at my own pace with just one advisory.

"If there's any emergency, come ring the bell," he said, "because everybody runs to it."

I didn't bother. Mean, green envy is a problem, but it isn't an emergency.

IF YOU GO...

For information on Stout's Lodge, call (800) 690-2650, or write Box 2010, Mikana, WI 54857. Its web site is www.stoutslodge.com.

7
ROLLING DOWN THE RIVER ROAD
BALLTOWN, IOWA

A LONG DAY'S DRIVE WAS ALMOST DONE when I climbed onto a stool at Breitbach's, a bar and restaurant filled on every floor with memorabilia and antiques, one of whom eventually turned my way and said, "Crops good down your way?"

I allowed as how they were. Not entirely bluffing, either. I covered farming long enough to learn the trick of talking corn and beans, though my coveralled companion's knowledge was genetic, passed down from a grandfather who had come to farm in eastern Iowa in 1864.

So we talked about the harvest—great yields, maybe records—and prices. In the toilet, of course, because a farmer can stand only so much good news. Ours was a talk as ingrained in corn country culture as you'll ever find and it took place in an apt setting. Breitbach's is the oldest bar in all of Iowa, opened in 1852 by federal permit approved by President Millard Fillmore, and thus the historically appropri-

ate place to end a harvest day's drive down a stretch of Iowa's Great River Road.

Corn and hogs and a cold one. Perfect.

I'd begun early in the day in Marquette and its bluff-side sister, McGregor. Marquette once was known as the western end of the famed—at least in bridge circles—Lawler Pontoon Bridge across the Mississippi River, but today is better known as the berth of the riverboat casino *Miss Marquette*.

McGregor also was born out of man's need to cross the Big Muddy. It was called MacGregor's Landing when Alexander MacGregor (somewhere the spelling changed) opened a ferryboat service in 1837.

The crossing was the gateway to the northern frontier and McGregor prospered. At its peak, it was home to 5,500 residents, though it later lost both population and importance.

But anyone who was anyone then passed through McGregor. The American House, built in 1854, was one of the first permanent hotels on the upper Mississippi, hosting guests such as Mark Twain, Ulysses S. Grant, Jefferson Davis and—a century later—President Jimmy Carter when he passed through on the *Delta Queen*. At one time, it was a bawdy house but today it is a bed and breakfast inn, tourism having replaced the world's oldest profession as an economic linchpin.

While in McGregor, I checked out the former home and office of "Diamond Jo" Reynolds, the onetime riverboat king, and a small house on the edge of town where one August Ringling once lived with his sons, who later moved to Wisconsin and worldwide circus fame.

It's hard to make time on the river road, but isn't that the point? A mile out of McGregor I stopped to hike in Pike's Peak State Park, the highest bluff on the Mississippi River and a wonderful spot to meditate on the magic of nature and the wide blue sky.

Named for the same Zebulon Pike who left his mark on a Colorado peak, the park's vistas are mesmerizing. Across the gorge of the great river is the confluence of the Mississippi and the Wisconsin River, its long journey now ended at Wyalusing State Park.

It was here that Marquette and Joliet arrived in 1673, becoming the first white men to lay their eyes on Iowa. The land later was owned by a grandniece of Alexander McGregor, who left it to the government in her will.

From Pike's Peak I headed south through the Iowa countryside. Sometimes the river disappeared from sight but would reappear around a curve or from hilltops that offered sweeping views of the land.

I stopped at a plain little country church which still identified itself as Norske Ev. Lutherske Kirke—1861. In Guttenberg, I stopped again to watch a barge move through Lock and Dam No. 10, one of the busiest gates on the upper river.

Merely watching is a respected pastime here. Ingleside Park stretches the length of the city along the river and bench after bench beckons visitors to sit and do nothing. Like someone has to twist my arm.

Once a camping spot for French explorers and for Sac and Fox Indians, Guttenberg was an important river town in the 1830s. But it truly blossomed in 1845 when a wave of German immigrants arrived. More than 100 stone buildings, many listed today on the National Historic Register, were built for shop and business owners, along with warehouses and hotels.

The city was named for—but spelled with an extra t— Johannes Gutenberg, noted inventor of movable type. A replica of his famous Gutenberg Bible is on display at the public library.

But time and daylight were running low and so I hurried south, through North Buena Vista with its hillside grotto, into Balltown and its historic bar. The business has been in Breitbach hands for six generations and over 100 years, and claims to be the only restaurant in the world visited by the outlaw Jesse James and the actress Brooke Shields, though not at a table for two.

Corn and hogs and a cold one. And a bonus. If you haven't had your fill of gorgeous river views already—and who could?—there's one inside Breitbach's.

The story goes that, in 1934, a band of gypsies straggled into Balltown asking for food but lacking money to order it.

But in exchange for a full belly, they said, their mural painter, Alberto, would paint a picture of the area's fabulous river view on a wall. A deal was struck. Alberto earned $15 and his fellow travelers ate for the two weeks he painted. Years later the painting was covered by paneling during some misguided remodeling, but in 1954 it was uncovered and restored and can now be seen from stools in the bar.

The Great River Road indeed.

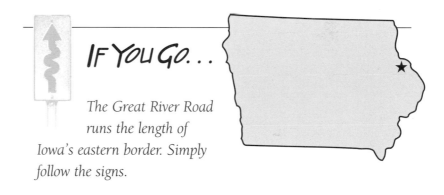

IF YOU GO...

The Great River Road runs the length of Iowa's eastern border. Simply follow the signs.

8
ALL FALLS DOWN

CRIVITZ, WISCONSIN

I HEARD THE TUMBLE-THUNDER OF VETERAN'S FALLS before its rushing water came into sight, and good for that.

To be absolutely honest I knew about where I was—in a great snowy woods in northeastern Wisconsin—but not precisely. I knew vaguely where I was headed—somewhere in the woods—but not exactly.

But details are for CPAs and doubt is for jurors. The timid are seldom disappointed but never surprised. I trudged boldly onward, guided only by Daniel Boone's theory that, hey, it has to be here somewhere.

Ask? you say.

Me? A man?

Besides, I'd just been given semi-directions without having to beg them. Several miles back two men had stopped next to my car while I puzzled over highways signs and wondered just what it was I couldn't seem to find. Mighty neighborly.

Can you get to the falls in winter, I asked. The older fellow glanced at the younger, thinking that's a new one on me. Most people go in summer.

No, he said. You'll get stuck. But I said, no, I mean walking, not driving, and he allowed as how that might work. So they pointed me in the direction of Veteran's Memorial Park where I strapped on snowshoes and set off, at first uncertainly but eventually toward the waterfall's roar.

I didn't, thankfully, get stuck.

I did, however, have to break trail through elbow-deep drifts of the deserted park to the Thunder River, threw a shoe I had to return and retrieve from the steep slope and finally slipped and slid and slithered to the edge of Veteran's Falls.

You're wondering how I knew it was elbow deep? One guess.

A lot more exciting than a summer visit, I'd say.

Marinette County is blessed with free-flowing water hell-

bent on hustling downstream, which gives rise to its boast of being Wisconsin's waterfall capital.

Other places have higher falls but few have rapids and falls in this number, from Dave's Falls, Long Slide and Smalley Falls, in the eastern half of the county, to Veteran's, McClintock and Strong Falls in the western half, not to mention Twelve Foot Falls and Horseshoe Falls in between. I'd visited some of them in summer, I figured one idle day, so why not in winter?

The eastern falls are reached from busy Highway 141. The western falls are linked by winding Parkway Road, alias Rustic Road 32, which is a bonus by any measure.

A road that is rustic in summer is rustic and then some in the off-season, starting with remote and bordering on lonely. Parkway Road stretches for dozens of miles through Marinette County's vast pine forests, which open occasionally to reveal frozen lakes and river vistas. Even if you aren't sure where you are going, this is the way to go.

There was fresh snow, but plows had been out and the going was only dicey in spots, like the curve where my car slid a bit toward a sign that read "Dead End." Very funny. From Veteran's Park, the road wound to the north along the Peshtigo flowages where cabins and resorts were shuttered for the quiet season. There were so few people around that when

I came upon a pair of walkers I gave them the country wave, palm on the wheel, fingers only raised in greeting. They seemed grateful just to have someone to wave back at.

It was a day that could have been improved by sunshine—what day couldn't?—but was otherwise comfortable. To reach the rapids at McClintock County Park I walked to the river under an archway of cathedral pines and suffered winter's soft and silent artillery barrage, big clumps of fresh snow that dropped branch by branch and burst against the ground.

Not incoming, only downcoming. Once, down my neck.

Rushing water is a comforting sound, as riveting for the ear as flickering fire is to the eye. Up the road again in Goodman County Park, the Peshtigo River flowed over rocks and under icy snowcaps, past empty cabins and the snow-covered "don't-do-this" and "don't-even-think-about-it" signs that parks can't be without.

But except for the rush and ripple of the dark river it was ghostly quiet and ghostly white. The park had snuggled under winter's snowy comforter and was content to rest, an odd visitor notwithstanding. This odd visitor certainly didn't mind.

There weren't enough hours in the day to visit all the falls, but I pressed on to Twelve Foot Falls, a few miles south of Dunbar. The drops so striking in summer were a bit hidden by snow and ice but its water bubbled on toward nearby Horseshoe Falls, which is off a path that can be rough in summer, let alone in the deep of winter.

And in approaching darkness to boot.

No matter. There was a reason Pope Gregory, when he came up with the modern calendar, followed each day with another.

Gregory was a waterfall fan. He knew that every day the water goes somewhere, but it never goes away. I'll be back.

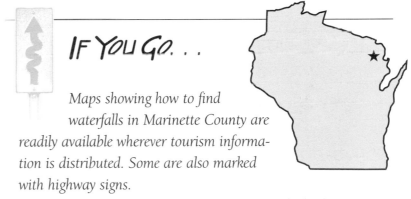

IF YOU GO. . .

Maps showing how to find waterfalls in Marinette County are readily available wherever tourism information is distributed. Some are also marked with highway signs.
And as long as you will be in the neighborhood, check out the historic lumber community of Goodman, where I went to find warmth and found something more—the next story.

9
THE COMPANY CLUBHOUSE

GOODMAN, WISCONSIN

I CAME IN FROM THE COLD TO FIND SOMETHING WET, and someplace warm.

I found it at the Goodman Clubhouse. Even better, it came with a side of history, a tour of Goodman's woodsy glory days, preserved today thanks to John and Claudia Moritz's second thoughts.

When they came to inspect the building for its business potential a few winters back, they found a place in need of shoring up and squaring off, in need of major renovation but not before unfortunate changes of the past were undone. In short, a huge job.

"Our first reaction was no," said John Moritz. "That was on a Saturday, but then we got up the next day and decided we'd like to try it."

After more than three years of hard labor, the rathskeller bar and restaurant were open and the former movie theater had been converted into a ballroom.

The company is dead. Long live the company town.

Wisconsin had its share of company owned-and-operated towns when mining and lumbering were roaring. It often served an employer's needs to provide housing and other services to attract workers, but while the booms were good times in one-industry towns, the busts were painful, often fatal.

Only a few towns survived their companies, said Randall Rohe, a University of Wisconsin-Waukesha professor with an interest in such communities. Goodman was a survivor, in large part because it was a model company town from birth.

It grew up around a mill built by the Goodman Lumber Company, which wanted to salvage millions of feet of white pine damaged in a 1907 fire. The company also purchased other large tracts of land here in Marinette County and in Florence and Forest Counties.

A number of Goodmans were involved, but the major figure here was Robert B. Goodman, who may have been a true lumber baron but was far from the rapacious, clear-cut school known for leveling northern forests and walking away.

He had studied timber science and forest management at Yale and in Europe. He would go on to serve on the Wisconsin Conservation Committee, help develop the Wisconsin Forest Crop Law and win honorary degrees from Syracuse and Wisconsin. He pioneered sustained growth lumbering; even the former head of the Wilderness Society credited him with "what they used to call a social conscience."

It extended from the forest to his town. The sawmill needed workers; workers needed housing. In 1908 construction began and in just a few years a clearing in the virgin forest was turned into a thriving community with more than 100 houses, a hotel, company store, office, bank, schools and, of course, a Soo Line Railroad station.

Many buildings were brick, heated by steam piped underground from the mill. Employees rented houses from the company, which also issued its own form of money to be used at the company store. Workers who ran short between paydays could get the company's brass coins in advance, an obvious drawback being that future wages could be gone before they were earned.

Catching up was difficult—remember the man who owed his soul to the company store?—but such dependence was common in company towns. Some felt a sense of servitude.

In 1913 work began on the building central to it all, the clubhouse. Goodman's bank had been designed by Holabird and Roche, a Chicago architectural firm that also designed such landmarks as Chicago's city hall, the Tribune and McCormick buildings. The designers wanted the clubhouse to resemble Washington's Mount Vernon.

It boasted an auditorium, theater with stage, social room, buffet room, lockers with showers, bowling alley, rathskeller and post office. On January 1, 1914, it opened with a dinner and dance that drew 600 people, Rohe said.

It only added class to what The American Lumberman had earlier called "perhaps the model woodsman's home of the United States." Some called it "the garden city of the Soo."

The Goodman Company practiced selective logging to preserve the life of the resource and operated into the 1950s, but the deaths of senior family members led to its sale in 1955, the first of several transfers. More important, new owners sold the company-owned businesses. The company town was on its own.

Succeeding decades were hard on Goodman. Fire took the mill (a veneer factory continues to operate) and down times took their toll. Unemployment rose, the population declined, some company-built houses were lifted up and moved away. The onetime company store was closed, and the bank became a branch of an out-of-town owner.

But the Goodman Clubhouse is back. The downstairs bar has expanded into the old bowling alley, fake ceilings have been removed and, Moritz said, future work will be in the spirit of the original design.

"The building was put together real well," he said. "Different people come in and tell me bits and pieces about the town and the same with this building, so you start to get a picture of what it was like."

So much so that he makes this offer:

"Any time anyone comes in with a Goodman Lumber Company coin I'll honor it at face value," he said. "Even double face value."

Alas, no one has come in to redeem old company coins. The offer still stands.

IF YOU GO. . .

The Fireside Lounge and Supper Club in the Goodman Clubhouse is open for dining and special events. For information, call (715) 336-2316.

10
HE-MEN TO SHE-MEN

ST. GERMAIN, WISCONSIN

WINTERS IN NORTHERN WISCONSIN CAN GET LONG, lonely and loony. Even knowing that doesn't prepare a stranger in St. Germain for the pictures on the wall at Eliason's Someplace Else supper club and bar.

The photos are undeniable proof that when an Up North winter begins to drag, so do the men about town. I mean, where but here in Vilas County can it be said that the male civic leaders are ordinary folks who put on their panty hose one leg at a time—right after they shave their beards.

Lest you get the wrong impression be assured that St. Germain is really a wonderful place and the annual Stump Dump Queen contest is merely a way to liven up the long month of February and raise some money for a local charity.

And liven the woods, it does.

A few months before I found the photos on the wall, 750 people had turned out to watch grown men parade in dresses and wigs, competing for the coveted Stump Dump Queen

crown. What started as a skit for the community's annual festival had become the main event, a weird but far from wicked night of wine, (wo)men and song.

Whatever else it might appear to be, "It's just plain fun, is what it is," insisted Jerry Eliason, a former queen.

Fun? You bet. Picture the 230-pound Eliason in the Sears lingerie department looking for black, rose-patterned, queen-sized panty hose.

"When I stretch these over me," Eliason told the startled young clerk, "every rose is going to be a bouquet."

Fun? You should have seen the night three snowmobilers entered Marv Doering's bar and saw the owner (another wanna-be queen) in costume. They looked at him, they looked at each other—and they looked for the door.

The first year, in the mid-1980s, contestants were afraid everyone would head for the door when 11 men "dressed up" for their skit. Eliason says someone had suggested that men in dresses would be pretty funny. The really funny thing was that 11 men agreed.

"Now that I think back, it was really a riot," he recalls. "We didn't know if we'd get 10 people. We only had chairs for 50 (and) 250 people showed up. We just modeled is all we did. We marched up on stage and showed a little leg, and it was just solid flashbulbs."

Well, a star was born—or 11 stars. Except for a few changes the cast has remained mostly intact through the years, but the show has grown into the social event of the winter in Vilas County. The contestants now go to great lengths to select just the right costumes: trash with flash, you might say. They even got professional help from a trained beautician who comes in to do their wigs and makeup.

"Now it takes two hours to get us ready," Eliason said. But it wasn't clear if that included the cocktail hour that seemed to be as important a part of preparation as fake eyelashes and nails.

It is said that one contestant's wife complained, after her husband had had a wee bit too much bottled courage, about how difficult it was to get a man out of a bra and girdle to put him to bed.

After a few years, organizers added a 32-foot lighted runway. Now each show has a theme—Hollywood stars or a Miss Universe contest, for example—and the men (or women, or whatever they are) have their music specially prepared.

One year the Stump Dump Queen theme was She-Haw, which meant poor Gary Frank had a problem again. He was going as one of the Judds, the look-alike mother and daughter act, and they didn't wear beards.

"I tried to disguise it the first four years I was in," he said. "One year I was Miss Piggy and I got to wear a mask, and one year I was a belly dancer so I got to wear a veil." But another year Frank was Janis Joplin and the growth that some say he was born with came off.

For the country show, contestants were expected to include Patsy Cline, Kitty Wells and Dolly Parton, of course, who had won the title before. That was in 1987, a year after Eliason won honors for his rendition of Miss Iceland. One year, Liza Minnelli walked off with the crown.

The competition is fierce, although the boys have a big collection of jewelry that they share. They pretty much keep their own stockings and other dainties, however. One year, a contestant had a wig flown in from Los Angeles. But not Gary Frank. He prefers to shop for his "womanly things" at the thrift shop in Eagle River.

Glen Giese, the owner of a local restaurant, says it's scary but some of the boys actually can look quite beautiful. He swears that one year a queen candidate who will go unnamed here looked so good that "if the guy was sitting over here, you'd be buying him drinks. Good god, he had a big red hat on and a dress, he looked beautiful. When he came out, his wife started getting clammy." Just like the snowmobilers, I bet.

Postscript....

The Stump Dump Queen pageant is still going strong. A recent theme was "Dude Looks Like a Lady." Eliason reports he was his usual beautiful self. Or her beautiful. Whatever.

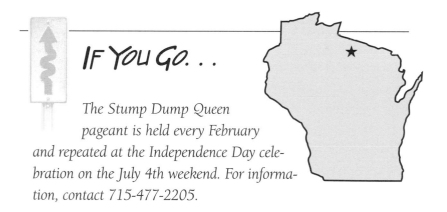

IF YOU GO. . .

The Stump Dump Queen pageant is held every February and repeated at the Independence Day celebration on the July 4th weekend. For information, contact 715-477-2205.

11
A GROWN-UP KID'S GARAGE

FOUNTAIN CITY, WISCONSIN

A TRIP THAT INCLUDED A LITTLE WORK AND A LITTLE GOLF (like there's any other kind?) needed a little culture, too, so I decided to take in one of the many little museums that dot this area like freckles on the Irish.

But which one? Maybe the Polk County Rural Life Museum in Balsam Lake, or the big Barron County Historical Society Museum in Cameron, or even the birthplace of Laura Ingalls Wilder in Pepin. A little work, a little golf, a little house.

Or maybe the Clear Lake Museum, which honors local heroes Gaylord Nelson, the longtime Democratic lion, and baseball pitcher Burleigh Grimes, spitballer extraordinaire. A place for a lefty and a righty I could have noted, if only I had gone there. In the end, I settled on Elmer's Museum, and yes, in part because any museum with a handle like that deserves a look-see.

The world-class collection of pedal cars was just gravy.

Elmer's is an occasional museum the way some chairs are occasional furniture. I mean, they're always furniture but they're only occasionally put to use, just as Elmer Duellman's barns are always filled with enough old toys to make Richie Rich jealous but are open to the public only part of the year. He needs the rest of the year to acquire new stuff, which Elmer admits has gotten easier now that people have figured out if they bring him something old and cool, he's just a boy who can't say no.

"I like everything old," said Duellman, "that's my problem."

This is not a man who should be permitted to view pyramids.

One version of how this all came about is that Duellman is filling out the childhood that shorted him years ago. He was born and raised here in this little town squeezed between the Mississippi River and its bluffs, one of eight children in a family without money for extras.

"All the kids were born in the house, and money was like zero," said his son, Rick. "There were no toys. Now he's making up for it."

Elmer doesn't get quite that Freudian, but doesn't help his own case when he admits, "It's exciting when you find a toy you've never seen before. Even still, it's neat."

The hard part is believing there are toys he's never seen before. Duellman started fixing bicycles at age 9, moved on to scooters and motorcycles and finally graduated to real cars, sometimes buying and selling but just as often keeping. As an adult, he opened an auto salvage yard, but at 22 he launched his second childhood by beginning to collect toys.

Actually, he wasn't a collector. He was a magnet.

At first he would go to local auctions and buy up all the toys. Why not? They were new to him, and if they were sturdy enough to have survived a child's use and abuse and still have some play in them, he figured they were worth collecting, too. He just hates these new plastic toys—temporary toys, most of them, that don't last a day beyond Christmas—but anything from the days when toys were toys is fine with him.

He has thousands on display now, from dolls to cars and trucks to tin windup toys, battery-operated action figures—you name it and Elmer likely has it. But his specialty is pedal cars, those little terrors of the sidewalk that resembled grown-up cars and trucks—some even had working lights and other parts—but which were small enough to be pedaled by their lucky kid owners.

He now has the world's largest collection, with hundreds on display and hundreds more stored in every available space on his property. Just before my visit, Duellman had come home from a collector's show in Iola with three more, including a 1935 "five-in-one" car that could be converted from an ambulance to a delivery truck to a wrecker to a dump truck and, finally, to a fire engine.

Duellman also has more than 100 full-size cars in his collection, many of them significant but none more so than the 1929 Ford Model A Phaeton that earned him national attention long before he opened his barns to the public.

That's because the Phaeton isn't in one of the barns. It's in the house, because what could a guy do when he comes home with two new antique cars for his own pleasure but his wife, upon seeing one, remarks that, oh honey, that one is pretty enough to go in the house. Elmer cut a hole in the family room wall, drove the car into the house and it's been there ever since.

For years, the cars and toys were mostly for personal

pleasure. Then the Buffalo County Historical Society asked to include his barns on a back roads tour and Elmer enjoyed it so much he decided to open it up occasionally, usually for a weekends in the fall. As a bonus, the museum is atop Eagle Bluff, the highest point along the Mississippi River.

Postscript....

After this column appeared in the newspaper I was flooded with calls from readers who had an old toy in the attic, or in the garage, or in the basement. Was it worth money? I couldn't help them with that, but I discovered later the place to find out was at the National Farm Toy Show. Read on.

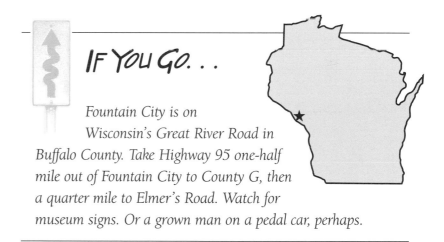

IF YOU GO. . .

Fountain City is on Wisconsin's Great River Road in Buffalo County. Take Highway 95 one-half mile out of Fountain City to County G, then a quarter mile to Elmer's Road. Watch for museum signs. Or a grown man on a pedal car, perhaps.

12
THE FARMER IN THE TOY BOX

DYERSVILLE, IOWA

BRUCE ASH, NO KID, IS EXPLAINING TO ME, no kid either, the finer points of slipping new toys—like the acres of farm toys that surrounded us—past a suspicious spouse's spending antennae.

First, don't even try.

"It's pretty damn tough," he said. "You buy a gift first, and promise you won't go to the bars for a month."

But even gift-wrapped sweet-talk and temporary temperance carry no guarantees.

"I bought one two or three years ago," Ash said, pointing to some pedal tractors nearby. "I paid $500 for it. My wife almost shot me."

She should have shot him later when he sold it again for $2,500. One of the pedal tractors he and a friend had brought to this show from Arcadia, Nebraska, a 1949 Massey Harris model manufactured in Dyersville in 1949, carried a price tag of $5,500. And while a couple of competitors thought that a

bit overpriced, Ash was certain the little tractor would fetch a big price before the weekend was over. The prey might be toys, but the estimated 15,000 to 20,000 "toy farmers" who flocked to Dyersville for the 20th Annual National Farm Toy Show take them very seriously.

As do toy makers. Gordy Schultz of Oshkosh, Wisconsin, started building formats from scratch in 1983, 1/64-scale models of tractors and planters, seeders, and combines, anything collectors wanted. A few years later he went full-time and now manufactures an estimated 5,000 pieces a year that sell at shows throughout the Midwest, though none as big as the national show.

Schultz is happy to be here even though he is relegated to a tent outside instead of the jammed main building.

"That's where I want to be, but I can't get in there," he said. "I've been on a list since 1990, but somebody has to die."

But outside would work. Schultz said a good show in Wisconsin might yield $600 to $700, but he was counting on $5,000 at Dyersville.

If not for farm toys, Dyersville would best be known as the home of the twin-spired Basilica of St. Francis Xavier and the cornfield set for the baseball fantasy "Field of Dreams."

But religion and Hollywood take a back seat to Fred Ertl's legacy in the eyes of grown boys. In 1945, then living in Dubuque and on strike, Ertl went into his basement and began tinkering with model tractors. Soon he began producing licensed replicas for John Deere and other major farm machinery manufacturers.

In the beginning farmers bought pedal tractors and smaller scale models for their children. As farming faded in numbers, both farmers and the citified sons and grandsons of farmers bought them out of nostalgia. A few were prescient enough to stick new toys away, still in boxes, and when toy collecting took off in the 1970s and '80s, they were in high corn—and had toy corn pickers to prove it.

Ertl eventually moved his manufacturing facility to Dyersville, which later became home to other farm toy producers and earned the reputation of "Farm Toy Capital of the World."

The National Farm Toy Museum, established in 1986 and open year-round, features more than 30,000 toys and exhibits over two floors. The first National Farm Toy Show, held in Dyersville in 1978, attracted 35 vendors and more than 1,500 shoppers. At this year's event, there were 279 open exhibitors, 41 outdoor sellers and 13 displays at various sites around town, including every classroom and hallway of the local high school. It shut down for the show, of course.

"This is the granddaddy of them all," Ash said, using language some of us reserve for the Rose Bowl. "It's a blast."

And it's a game. At one tent on Friday, hours before the show officially opened, a pedal tractor shopper from Ohio was doing the dickering dance with a vendor from Minnesota. The Ohio man didn't really need another toy; he had maybe 300 pieces at home. And the Minnesota man was a reluctant, but motivated, seller.

"I do a lot of traveling," the Minnesotan said. "And I love buying. The selling part I don't care about, but you have to do the selling to support the buying.

"The hunt," he said, "is the fun."

It's impossible to estimate how much money changes hands in the exhibit halls, tents and tailgates where deals are made. Some pieces go for a few bucks, others for $100 and $300 and a few go for a lot more than that. But multiply those numbers by 15,000 or so and you see how big the toy game has become.

"Oh my goodness," said Keri Wittmeyer, director of the Farm Toy Museum. "There are people spending hundreds and hundreds and thousands of dollars. They come in here with their wads of cash—I'm just amazed at the wads of cash—and their credit cards and they spend, spend, spend."

And more than a few take precautions. I told Wittmeyer about Ash's thoughts on grown boys' toys and marital harmony.

"You know," she said, "that's funny, because a lot of guys are buying things for their wives."

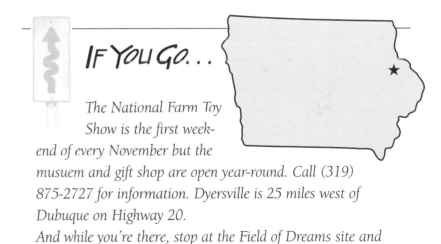

IF YOU GO...

The National Farm Toy Show is the first weekend of every November but the musuem and gift shop are open year-round. Call (319) 875-2727 for information. Dyersville is 25 miles west of Dubuque on Highway 20.

And while you're there, stop at the Field of Dreams site and run around the bases. It's worth the side trip.

13
A PATH BACK INTO HISTORY

HOLMEN, WISCONSIN

THE BRIDGE, AS MOST DO, HAD A WEIGHT LIMIT. FIVE.

Not five tons or five trucks, certainly not five parades with marching bands and elephants.

Five people. A jazz quintet. The Dionne quintuplets. A basketball team, but only the starters.

Once its back was strong. Ninety years ago the old bridge carried horses and wagons and loads of hay hauled by farmers who found it growing wild, and free, in the Black River bottoms. But time is as heavy a burden for old spans as it is for old backs, so as I approached the crossing on a late autumn afternoon just made for walking I double-checked. Concluding my lonesome self was four short of danger, I pressed on down McGilvray Road, the passageway time forgot but whose friends remembered.

Old roads need friends and a few years ago, McGilvray Road—the historic "Seven Bridges Road" that carried early travelers across this swampy stretch of La Crosse County—needed them desperately.

The road had existed, in various forms, since the 1850s, when a Scottish immigrant named Alexander McGilvray settled here and established a settlement, along with a ferry across the Black River. For nearly 40 years the ferry made seasonal crossings, despite occasional log jams, until residents finally petitioned for a bridge. In 1892 the first of a series of wooden structures was erected.

The marshy land was hard on wooden bridges, however, so between 1905 and 1908 the La Crosse Bridge and Steel Company erected a series of small bowstring arch-truss bridges that were quite advanced for the time. They were designed and patented by Charles M. Horton, who used "hook-slips" instead of rivets and bolts to make stronger connections.

Before the bridges were built, farmers would often cut hay in summer but wait until winter to retrieve it when they could haul a sleigh across the ice. That was a lot of trouble, but the hay—grown with the help of spring flooding that carried in water and nutrients—was worth it.

"The hay was so thick and so tall that I could walk through the meadow there and once you get into the mead-ow...you'll never see your feet until you come out because it's so thick," one farmer recalled years later. "It was a lot better than anything up here on the high ground."

After the bridges were built, farmers could go in with horses and wagons, hunters and fishermen found new access and carriages carried travelers along McGilvray Road to Trempealeau.

Eventually, however, better roads were built and McGilvray, with its narrow bridges, became the road less traveled. By the 1960s, the Department of Natural Resources was obtaining surrounding parcels for what became the Van Loon Wildlife Area and the main bridge over the Black River was removed. Fire claimed the long wooden bridge in 1985, about the time the Department of Transportation concluded the five remaining bowstring bridges had outlived their usefulness, were in unsafe condition and ought to be removed. The estimated cost was between $65,000 and $100,000.

If ever a road needed friends, that was the moment. When a few people who knew of the area learned of the state's plans, they decided to get involved. One of them, Dorothy Ann Ferguson, wrote to the local newspaper to rally support for the road.

"The trail of the historic truss bridges presented a majestic nature walk into the past," her letter said, "where you could feel you truly stepped back into history."

And so the Friends of McGilvray Road came to be. They convinced the state that money earmarked for bridge removal should be used for preservation and maintenance instead and set about to raise more funds, primarily by commissioning artists Michael Klafke and Arthur Anderson to paint pictures of the bridges and selling the prints. They sold 350 prints of the first painting at $80 and $100 a pop, and each of the successive prints sold about as well.

Eventually, the Friends of McGilvray Road had invested more than $200,000 in their road. A moving company was brought in to raise one bridge that had fallen in the water, and new abutments were installed on other spans where old ones had washed out. That still left them with a hole where the fifth bridge had been. But then the group found a historic bridge of roughly the same era, though of a different design, and had it transplanted from Pierce County.

"Seven Bridges Road" has only six bridges today—despite the modest weight limits on some, all are quite safe—but if the Big Ten can have 11 teams why sweat this math? Certainly not the Friends of McGilvray Road, who in 1997, gathered to formally dedicate and reopen their treasured pathway, which has been listed on both the state and national registers of historic places.

Today the road is a fine walking trail that runs about 3.5 miles round-trip through the Van Loon Wildlife Area to the river, where it dead-ends. It is used by hunters, hikers, fishermen, bird-watchers, outdoor photographers and others. The days when it carried early motor cars from La Crosse to Trempealeau are long gone, but the days when hikers might come across white-tailed deer or beavers on a late autumn afternoon just made for walking are back.

I don't know about you, but I call that progress.

IF YOU GO...

McGilvray Road is northwest of Holmen in western Wisconsin. Take Old Highway 93 west from Highway 53, turn right on Amsterdam Road and look for the entrance.

14
STORIES OF BUNNIES, BRAVERY

LANCASTER, WISCONSIN

A BURIAL PLACE CAN BE AS INTRIGUING FOR WHOSE BONES ARE NOT IN IT as for whose are. And it can be even more intriguing if a touch of mystery might have been interred with the last remains.

Grave matters, I know. But while in Grant County on business of quite a livelier nature I came across an example of each.

The former is in Lancaster's original cemetery, a small plot a block off the square where stands Grant County's historic courthouse with its Civil War memorial.

Most visitors, if they were interested at all, would seek out this cemetery because it is the last resting place of Nelson Dewey, the first governor of Wisconsin, who was buried near his sons, Charles "Little Charlie" Dewey and Orrin "My Brother" Dewey.

A state historical marker tells Dewey's particulars, but it takes a visit to the Cunningham Museum across the square to get the lowdown on the more interesting marker in that cemetery, a small white obelisk tucked in the shadow of the old Episcopal Church a few yards away.

It is oddly compelling on several levels. It is a Moslem marker, for one, in a small rural Wisconsin community.

And it honors a man who never set foot in Lancaster, nor likely anywhere else in America. But Sargeant Lastam, as the honored man is known, earned the tribute.

In 1910, in a jungle halfway around the world, he saved a Lancaster man's life. It only cost him his own.

Ted Lowry was the son of a prominent Lancaster lawyer, but an itch for adventure made him a career soldier who went wherever career soldiers were needed. In 1910 that was the Philippines, where Lowry was in charge of a native unit attempting to put down insurrections.

As Lowry later told the story, he was leading a group of men single file through the jungle when a hostile native stepped from behind a tree and drew back his arm.

Sargeant Lastam, as Lowry described the moment, rushed under Lowry's arm, took the knife meant for his commanding officer in his own chest and died in Lowry's arms.

Years later, Lowry died in a fall over a balcony rail at an American Legion dinner at the U.S. Embassy in Mexico City and was buried in the national cemetery at Arlington, Virginia. But long before that, he had erected the marker for Lastam in his family's old church cemetery in southwestern Wisconsin.

"Greater love had no man than this," it reads, "that a man lay down his life for a friend."

Nice story. It was at the Cunningham Museum—a fine, small town museum, by the way, and worth a visit for its exhibit on Grant County's long-gone black settlement—where I also found the tale of Laura Rountree Smith.

She was the granddaughter of John Hawkins Rountree, the pioneer founder of nearby Platteville.

Young Laura lived at the old Rountree residence—now the home of the University of Wisconsin-Platteville's chancellor—where she spent much of her time caring for her aged mother. Often she would sit and watch rabbits play in the yard of Duncan McGregor, then the president of the State Normal School.

One day, according to *Old Crawford History, Vol. 1*, Smith saw McGregor chase a rabbit from a flower bed and conceived the idea of children's stories written from the rabbits' point of view.

Of course, Flopsy, Mopsy, Cottontail and Peter—the rabbits that made Mr. McGregor famous—have long been credited to Beatrix Potter, an English writer who lived from 1866 to 1943. But many in Grant County, including the museum's director, Al Weber, believe Laura Rountree Smith was the actual creator.

Weber acknowledges the claim will spark an argument, and he has had several over it, but he believes Potter might have been unduly "inspired" by Smith's work. It is undisputed, at any rate, that Platteville had a Dr. McGregor who had rabbits in his yard; some even say the man pictured in Potter's book resembled the local McGregor.

Laura Rountree Smith wrote dozens of children's books, including *The Pixie on the Farm, Bunny Cotton Tail, Three Little Kittens Who Lost Their Mittens, The Pixie in the House, Bunny Bright Eyes,* and more.

Curiously, Laura, never blessed with strong health, and her infirm mother died within months of each other in 1924 and were buried in the family lot in Hillsdale Cemetery.

As *Old Crawford History* put it, "just when her works had gained national fame and demand, she was called upon to pay the debt of nature, passing away while engaged in some of her best work."

Weber's warning aside, I'm enough of a Wisconsin partisan to accept Smith as Peter Rabbit's real creator. The next morning I sought out her grave in Platteville, where a small flat marker gives Smith's name, dates of birth and death and adds simply, "Authoress."

I waited a few minutes, hoping maybe a rabbit would hop by and settle all doubt. But life isn't that tidy. Nor, obviously, is death.

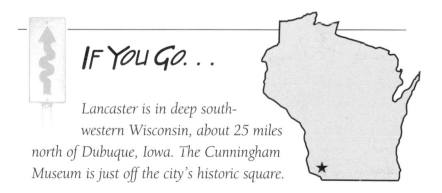

IF YOU GO. . .

Lancaster is in deep southwestern Wisconsin, about 25 miles north of Dubuque, Iowa. The Cunningham Museum is just off the city's historic square.

15
In Search of a Haven

South Haven, Michigan

AND A TIMELY HAVEN IT PROVED TO BE, because road builder rage was setting in.

If I had a kid to counsel on a career I would say, "Boy (unless he was a girl), forget computers. Get yourself a job with a future. Learn road building and you'll never have to worry where your next meal's coming from."

Road builders rule. I left Milwaukee in high spirits on the first day of a leisurely circle of Lake Michigan, because after all these years of gazing across the broad water and wondering what was there, it was time to stuff a bag with shirts and shorts and check it out.

But the drive through Illinois was a torturous maze of tollbooths and brake lights, of dodging barrels like a rodeo cowboy and more flashers than a pervert convention.

Indiana was little better, especially the unintended tour of beautiful downtown Gary. It was a long day of detours and rising temperatures, inside and out, of oaths and deprecations for which I now apologize, and I was as happy to reach the harbor town of South Haven, Michigan, as any steamer captain who ever sought shelter from a Great Lakes storm. Within minutes I was at the Old Harbor Inn, where my quiet room overlooked the pleasure boats on the Black River, the channel that links South Haven's busy marina with Lake Michigan.

Ahhh.

South Haven's lake breezes and long sandy beaches have been knocking the rough edges off modern life since before life was modern. In the 1870s, South Haven was a bustling village of fishermen and lumbermen, and the first orchards and gardens of today's still-vibrant fruit industries were already established. Then resorts began to appear. The first opened for summer tourists in the 1880s and by 1902, South Haven was home to 215 resorts and hotels.

All were serviced by passenger steamers at first, until

roads were built from Chicago to carry automobiles on the 130-mile trip. Eventually roads became so good that travelers went elsewhere for summer rest and recreation, leaving South Haven's tourism business in decline, but in recent years the lure of the lake has renewed the tourism industry in South Haven and many other communities up and down the shore.

South Haven has about 6,000 year-round residents but as many as 15,000 during summer months. Many of the original resorts, large Victorian homes with lake views, have been converted to bed and breakfast inns. Many beach cottages and condominiums are also available for rent, in addition to full-service hotels.

Amid the new bustle, South Haven's maritime heritage remains evident.

The city's signature structure is its South Pierhead Lighthouse, a 35-foot steel cylindrical tower that was built in 1903, replacing a slightly taller wooden tower that had been guiding ship captains through fog and darkness since 1872.

The pier, now a 1,200-foot concrete walkway, has been extended several times through the years. But even in shorter incarnations it tested the constitution of lighthouse keepers during blustery weather. The longest-serving keeper was one James Donahue, who lost a leg in the Battle of the Wilderness in 1864 but who was fitted with a wooden replacement on which he stumped back and forth to the light for many years.

His journal showed that lighthouse duty at a remote outpost was not always berry-picking and picnicking. On April 4, 1887, he wrote, "I started the light at Sundown. In going to the light I was knocked down with flying ice and come-ing back I was struck on the hip and shoalders. I am not able to walk this morning."

South Haven's maritime past is especially evident when tall ships visit the harbor during summer months. The turnout can rival that for South Haven's biggest weekend of the year—the annual National Blueberry Festival each August.

Festival features range from such events as a blueberry bubblegum contest to a blueberry pie-eating contest, which is not all that big a range when you think about it. There is also blueberry bingo, a blueberry queen and blueberry parade over which she presides.

Fruit is big business in Michigan. Blueberries, strawberries and cherries are available at roadside stands or at u-pick-'em patches. South Haven is also peach country. Peach varieties like Halehaven, Kalhaven, Redhaven, Fairhaven and more were developed here during decades of research by Michigan State University experts, and some South Haven varieties became widely planted around the world.

Fishing charters and other boat rentals are available at South Haven. The community's tidy downtown and riverfront include a number of shops that are not overly tacky, by resort standards.

In the evening I had dinner aboard the *Idler*, a riverboat restaurant and bar moored at Nichols Landing adjacent to my hotel.

The *Idler* was built a century ago by Lafayette Lamb, son of a wealthy Iowa lumberman. Lamb would take the *Idler*, guided by her companion towboat the *Wanderer*, from New Orleans in the winter to cooler ports in summer. In 1904 the *Idler* was taken to St. Louis for the World's Fair.

Early this century, the *Idler* was purchased by V. L. Price of Clinton, Iowa, the father of actor Vincent Price. V. L. Price used the *Idler* for entertaining—completely rebuilding it after a devastating fire in 1920—for 58 years until he sold the boat to Nabisco. In 1981 a South Haven family obtained the *Idler* and converted her to a floating restaurant.

And so ended a hectic day on a most peaceful note, with red snapper and red wine on a riverboat that rocked every so gently in its berth. There wasn't an orange barrel in sight. I decided this journey would be all right.

Postscript...

And it was. More adventures from my circle tour are coming up.

IF YOU GO. . .

For information on South Haven, contact the Convention and Visitors Bureau, 415 Phoenix Street, South Haven, Michigan 49090; 1-800-SO-HAVEN. Or www.southhaven.org.

16
THE VICTORIAN PORT CITY

MANISTEE, MICHIGAN

FAR FROM HOME, OR WAS I? Moseying up Lake Michigan's far shore I checked into a small, Cream City brick hotel built by German immigrants, and thus upheld more than a century of Manistee tradition. Where would any true Milwaukeean lay his noggin for a night but at the city's oldest hotel, the Milwaukee House?

Home, away from home.

Milwaukee and Manistee (not to be confused with Manistique, in the Upper Peninsula) were forever linked by the long-gone steamers that once connected lakeshore ports.

As early as the 1850s, but especially in later decades, German immigrants from Milwaukee crossed Lake Michigan to work in the bustling timber and sawmill village.

Manistee was something in those days. More than 25 mills operated then, producing as much as 300 million board feet of lumber a year, enough for 30,000 houses. One mill had the capability to saw 24 boards at one time, and by 1885

Manistee produced more shingles than any other city in the world. At the turn of the century there were more than a dozen millionaire lumbermen in Manistee.

Some Milwaukeeans had business connections here. Val Blatz, for example, owned saloons in Manistee, and local lumber baron Delos Filer also owned an interest in a Milwaukee sawmill machinery factory. But a community so dependent upon wood, and inevitably burdened with a mountain of scrap, was also a community waiting to burn. On October 8, 1871, the same day killing fire raged through Chicago and Peshtigo, Wisconsin, the spark was lit and 75 percent of Manistee burned to the ground.

The city rebuilt, this time with brick. And more than 80 percent of the brick came from Milwaukee, including that used for Charlie Dieffenbach's new hotel and tavern at the end of River Street. On December 1, 1874, the new hotel celebrated its founding with a grand ball, and early in 1875 it opened for business.

The old papers tell of the occasional liquor-related dust-up, but Charlie apparently ran a respectable establishment. In 1892 the *Manistee Times and Standard* reported Dieffenbach had just slaughtered a 475-pound hog from which 125 pounds of lard was extracted.

"If animals fare so well at Charlie's hands," the paper noted, "his boarders must live on the fat of the land."

With its hometown name, the Milwaukee House was a draw for German workers. But as lumbering declined, Manistee's millionaire heyday waned, and when the hotel closed in 1922 it served mostly as a storage building until Charles Hedstrom, a local man who had gone on to work in radio and as a NBC television producer, returned with big ideas. About the time

Manistee began to reinvent itself to reflect its former Victorian glory, Hedstrom began to restore the Milwaukee House as well.

Originally offering 30 rooms—"about the size a monk would sleep in," Hedstrom said—it now offers eight elegantly furnished guest rooms, along with a solarium and patio. Antiques are everywhere. And if Hedstrom is raising prize hogs there in the tradition of the original owner they escaped my attention.

Manistee bills itself as "The Victorian Port City," a boast that has the blessings of the National Register of Historic Places. The entire downtown shopping district is on the register, as are most of the 24 stately "Painted Ladies" on a window-peeking walking tour of the onetime millionaires' homes.

Even the fire station, a gloriously bright pink fire hall with copper-domed tower, is on the register. Michigan's oldest continuously used station is still, as it was described in 1888, "a credit to the city." Even the brass pole that leads to upstairs sleeping quarters is still in use.

Another architectural highlight is the Ramsdell Theater, where Manistee residents like to brag that the actor James Earl Jones, who grew up nearby, got his start as a stage carpenter.

Thomas Jefferson Ramsdell, pioneer lawyer and civic leader, was laughed at by the lumber barons' wives when he announced plans for a grand theater, but he found his revenge in a large mural that featured nude women—whose faces were those of the lumber barons' wives.

Visitors can tour Manistee's historic hot spots by trolley, or ride the Manistee River on a floating taxi called the *Water Bug*. The city has also developed a long river walk that runs more than a mile from the downtown to Lake Michigan.

Manistee is the third largest oil-producing area of Michigan and remains a major salt producer. The Briny building, once noted for salt and mineral baths thought to have the power to cure all manner of ills, has been renovated. And Manistee is also home to a prominent fiberglass casket maker whose specialty is personalizing vaults with the logo of the deceased's alma mater.

A popular fishing center, Manistee also offers two broad, sandy lakefront beaches for sunbathers and Orchard Beach State Park, originally a playground for sawmill workers, for campers.

Each September Manistee hosts the Victorian Port City Festival, highlighting its historic architecture, and the first weekend of December the city fills for an old-fashioned Victorian Christmas parade, which includes lighted holiday trees pulled behind horse-drawn sleighs.

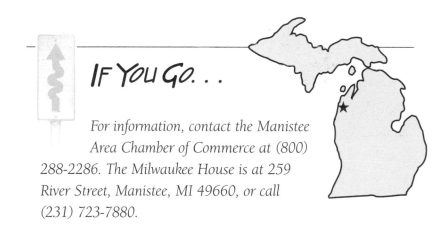

IF YOU GO. . .

For information, contact the Manistee Area Chamber of Commerce at (800) 288-2286. The Milwaukee House is at 259 River Street, Manistee, MI 49660, or call (231) 723-7880.

17
TRAVERSE GRAND, EVEN IN RAIN

OLD MISSION, MICHIGAN

THE NIGHT SKY HAD BEEN A CELESTIAL CENTERFOLD. A silver curl of moon peeked through flecks of gray and black and the last pink-orange traces of a fallen sun. Twice beautiful it was, first in its rightful place and then again splashing off the surface of Traverse Bay.

The morning after was gray and dark, a big wet bruise of a daybreak, but the rain did keep the jet ski hooligans in bed to dream dreams of disruption and gave me time to plan the next episode in my circle of Lake Michigan.

Golf, you're probably thinking. I've let slip my love for the devil's game and this part of Michigan, first the nation's cherry capital, has now become the nation's Golf Coast. From Traverse City to Petoskey, from Boyne to Gaylord, courses are strung together like pearls around Winnie (Mrs. Arnold) Palmer's neck.

It is a 100-course meal, enough to sate the hungriest hacker and every layout grander than the one before. But I couldn't play golf on a workday.

Not two days in a row.

I had thought a ride on a tall ship would be fun. The two-masted schooner *Malabar* has been based in Traverse City since 1987, offering daily sails on West Grand Traverse Bay. The *Malabar* is also a floating bed and breakfast, either topside under the stars or in staterooms, but, like Gilligan, I would have settled for a three-hour cruise.

Not in the rain, though, which also ruled out renting a small boat and weighed against beach-and-book time or dune hiking.

To Old Mission, then, for a taste of Door County, a taste of France, a taste of wine. Maybe several.

Old Mission Peninsula is the sloping, scenic 18-mile tongue that divides Grand Traverse into east and west bays. The highway affords stunning views of orchards and water, sometimes rising on great hogbacks to reveal hillsides falling off sharply to water both east and west. Whiplash is a danger.

The tip of the peninsula—site of Old Mission Lighthouse, not far from the namesake Indian mission established by the Reverend Peter Dougherty—lies on the 45th parallel, midway between the North Pole and the Equator.

So is the Bordeaux region of France, so no coincidence that vast orchards and vineyards sprawl across these fertile hillsides. Forty percent of the nation's tart cherries are grown in Michigan, although again this year the price paid growers will trail the cost of production, a dilemma even farmers can't make up in volume.

If discouraged, they can drown their sorrows. I visited Old Mission Market, where Peninsula Cellars offers wine tasting, and found nice dry white wines in addition to the sweet fruit wines common in such areas. It was the same at other wineries, but not so many that I couldn't safely resume my circle study.

With regrets at having to miss the popular Leelanau Peninsula, I headed toward Petoskey, stopping at Charlevoix to watch the Beaver Island ferry load and to marvel at so much wealth.

A port community of postcard beauty, Lake Charlevoix was Ernest Hemingway's boyhood summer spot. Beaver Island, a 32-mile ferry ride away, was where Wisconsin's James Jesse Strang, a self-appointed Mormon leader who also had himself crowned a "king," took his flock of followers in the 1840s.

With mixed success. Strang acquired numerous wives, but his aggressive nature made enemies, some of whom assassinated him in 1856. Several of Strang's wives brought him back to Wisconsin for burial.

A few miles up the shore was Bay Harbor, site of an ultra-upscale golf and recreation development where some homesites start at $1 million. And don't even ask about green fees, although I foolishly did. A twilight nine holes at the best course was a larcenous $100.

Petoskey, a handsome community with tasteful shops and stately homes, drew its name from early landowner Ignatius Petosegay, apparently a phonetic speller. But I spent the night in historic Bay View, an adjoining community with an intriguing history still much in evidence.

In 1875, a group of Methodists formed a camp meeting here "for intellectual and scientific culture and the promotion of the cause of religion and morality," most notably temperance.

They first used tents for their preaching and lectures. After railroad service arrived the next year, Bay View blossomed. Within ten years, summer cottages, a hotel, chapel and other buildings were in place and such notables as Frances Willard, Booker T. Washington and William Jennings Bryan came for Chautauqua-style events.

Eventually more than 400 Victorian summer homes were built here and many are still owned by descendants of the builders. Today old Bay View, still host to a popular summer music program, is a thriving seasonal community and a designated National Historic Landmark. Homes, privately owned, can only be occupied from May until October; the Bay View Association sets all rules.

One is that no alcohol can be sold at places such as the historic Stafford's Bay View Inn where I stayed. It didn't mean the inn couldn't provide wine in guest rooms, as it did, or that guests couldn't bring wine to dinner, as some did. But guests who so much as stepped off the gracious porch with drink in hand were immediately reminded of the rules.

I'm a sucker for history, so I walked around soaking it in.

On the front of one house a sign noted that "Margaret Mitchell completed *Gone With the Wind* here. Published 1936."

I wondered if Bay View would someday post a sign saying "Dennis McCann completed *A Monk Swimming* here in 1998." But my wife said I probably had to write a good book, not just read one.

IF YOU GO. . .

This story was part of an exploration of Lake Michigan's shoreline. While all of the little communities mentioned have their own tourism publications, the most comprehensive sources of Lake Michigan circle tour information would be the Michigan Travel and Tourism Department, (800) 644-8644, and Great Lakes Circle Tour, Reliving History Along Lake Michigan's Circle Tour Route, *by Bob and Ginger Schmidt (Amherst Press, (800) 333-8122).*

18
HORSES RULE THE ROAD

MACKINAC ISLAND, MICHIGAN

IN 1898 ISLAND RESIDENTS HAD HAD IT UP TO HERE (think chin-high) with noisy, smoky horseless carriages that frightened the bejabbers out of hardworking horses and threatened the life and limb of pedestrians.

So on July 6, 1898, the village council peered into the future, decided it could live quite well without such modern contraptions and banned them.

My kingdom for a Ford? In Detroit, maybe, but not here. And after a century of car-free living there are no regrets, certainly not from bike-rental interests.

On July 6, 1998, reenactors ferried a single car to the island (a 1901 steam-powered horseless carriage, naturally) and paraded it through the village to the courthouse, where descendants of the 1898 council and members of the 1998 council reread the original ban.

The car was then removed by horse-drawn dray, assuring that now and forever Mackinac will be the ultimate getaway for upscale Amish, free of parking meters, gas pumps and road rage, except among those who fail to watch where they step. So one summer day I left my car in Mackinaw City, boarded a tourist-clogged ferry and spent a few days on what a writer described in 1836 as "the wildest and tenderest little piece of beauty that I have yet seen on God's earth."

No disputing that. On a summer day when the sun is bright and warm, when the sky above and water below compete to be the prettiest blue, it's easy to see why armies long fought for control of Mackinac, even before fudge became an island staple.

Mackinac's story is America's story. Indians treasured it for its physical attractions, grew food here, buried their dead here.

The earliest missionaries—Father Marquette prominent among them—arrived at the Straits of Mackinac, where the great lakes Huron and Michigan meet, in the 1670s. Fur traders prospered in the 1700s. It was to protect the traders' interests that Fort Mackinac was built high on a bluff overlooking the straits and the busy docks, where agents of John Jacob Astor's American Fur Company shipped a fortune in hides to markets in Europe.

The island was a strategic military post. The British army reluctantly left Mackinac after Americans were granted control at the end of the Revolutionary War, but remained nearby.

At the outbreak of the War of 1812, the British and their Indian allies slipped back onto the island at what is now British Landing and sur-

prised the sleeping Americans, whose commander counted heads, saw he was outflanked and outnumbered and immediately surrendered.

American troops unsuccessfully tried to take the island in 1814, but only after the war's end did they again gain control by treaty. The Army remained until 1894; in 1895 the fort and surrounding park, which today includes about 82 percent of the island's land area, were placed under the administration of the Mackinac Island State Park Commission.

Such vast park holdings mean that Mackinac, though its business area is busy and crowded during peak tourism season, continues to have undeveloped spaces, quiet woods and vistas that should never be disturbed.

Cars aren't missed, either. Horse-drawn carriages, horse-drawn taxis, even a horse-drawn hearse serve most transportation needs, if somewhat slowly.

Saddle horses and self-drive carriages are available, and bicycles—1,220 rentals licensed by the village and 1,500 owned by residents and summer workers—swarm island roads like flies on unwatched potato salad.

I wanted the full island experience, so I nibbled on fudge, pedaled the eight-mile shore path to soak up the nonstop views, walked the high bluff streets to admire the grand, Victorian summer "cottages" built for wealthy families a century ago.

I spent—and that's the perfect verb—one night at the posh Grand Hotel, the famous summer hotel with the longest porch in the world, and views to match. I played the hotel's golf course, where the two nines are about a mile apart and golfers are toted from the ninth green to the tenth tee by horse-drawn golf cart.

And of course I took the carriage tour of island sites, inevitably stuck behind bratty kids whose mother thought them charming anyway and whose father looked like he would prefer to be somewhere, anywhere, else. Instead, he was on the front pew of a wagon with horses' hinders in his face and his own misbehaving kids at his side. Ah, the American vacation.

But the tour was fine, especially after I switched carriages during one stop. We passed the grand summer house of Michigan's governor and the barracks where visiting Boy or Girl Scout troops can stay. We passed Skull Cave, where Indians long buried their dead, much to the dismay of a

British soldier who sought refuge one night on a bed of skulls. We visited Arch Rock, a geological curiosity, stopped at the fort and rolled past island cemeteries and churches, all to the accompaniment of the driver's patter.

So cars aren't missed. Horses are dependable, though they do have leaky radiators and backfire a bit.

Unless you've been on the tour, you heard it here first.

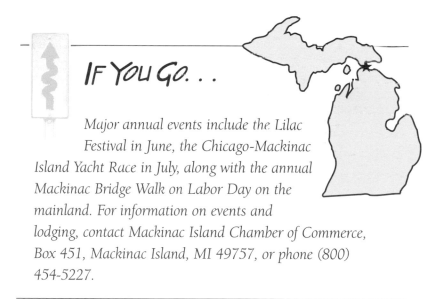

IF YOU GO...

Major annual events include the Lilac Festival in June, the Chicago-Mackinac Island Yacht Race in July, along with the annual Mackinac Bridge Walk on Labor Day on the mainland. For information on events and lodging, contact Mackinac Island Chamber of Commerce, Box 451, Mackinac Island, MI 49757, or phone (800) 454-5227.

19
CABIN FEVER IN GAYS MILLS

GAY MILLS, WISCONSIN

FEWER AND FEWER MEMORIES REACH TO CABIN DAYS, but Denny Lund remembers.

He remembers the backbreaking work, the sweat and heat of summer that made the logs heavier than they ought to be, and the work harder.

And that was just 20 years ago, in the ranch house era.

The work isn't any easier today, but Lund and others are back working with log cabins, the same historic structures he worked on as a high school senior because the work didn't get done then. Maybe this time it will.

"We hope so," he said. "We have a long row to hoe."

Some dreams survive their dreamer. For years before her death in 1994, it was the dream of Leita Slayton to establish a settlement of historic log buildings in a village park here. Much of her hope was realized.

With the help of the local historical society, log cabins were found in the hills and valleys of Crawford County and then disassembled, trucked to Gays Mills and rebuilt. Each was from the 1800s, including one known as the "McCann cabin," which was lure enough to bring me to apple country.

Much of the original work was done by volunteers. Other labor came from paid workers like Lund, whose summer job on a cabin crew was funded with a government grant. He helped move the one-room log schoolhouse from Wauzeka Ridge to the village park.

"A lot of hard work," he said. "I remember I sweated a lot."

A village of eleven buildings was planned, but only eight were moved before the project slowed and finally ground to a halt. And the museum-like attraction Slayton had hoped to create to bring visitors to Gays Mills was never fully developed. For some years the buildings just sat, fragile curiosities subject to the whims of time and weather.

Finally, it was decision time.

formed and, most important, a new energy discovered or, in some cases, recaptured.

"I guess the biggest reason (I came back) is I did work on it 20 years ago and it was hard work," said Lund, who with his wife, Kathy, co-chairs the Log Cabin Heritage Society. "I don't want to see all that fall apart."

So much would be lost, because these cabins, small and plain as they appear, represent those who settled this rugged corner of Wisconsin. Here is Henry Altenburg's log corncrib, built in Bush Hollow without the use of nails; Swiss settler Samuel Matti's corncrib and henhouse of butternut logs; and a granary owned by Norwegians Jens and Ragnild Nederlo and their children—no kidding here—Ole and Lena.

"Do we want to save these buildings or do we want them torn down?" was how village clerk Robin Eitsert put it.

The answer must have made Leita Slayton, now somewhere in the yonder, smile. Meetings were held, a new group

And here is the McCann cabin with its waterwheel. Alas, its condition is among the most fragile and the need for shoring up is urgent.

One version of the building's history spells the name "McCahn" but Jacob Vedvig, president of the Crawford County Historical Society, says McCann is correct.

It was built with dovetailed corner notches characteristic of Norwegian construction for immigrant Ingebret Peterson, who homesteaded in Copper Creek Valley in the 1850s. It takes its name from John J. McCann, whose wife Mary Bird had bought the granary from her mother. They had three children and, after their house burned around 1909, the family moved into the granary and made it their home. Vedvig, who lived nearby, said the story goes that Mary died in the loft and had to be removed by ladder, but their children lived on the land into the 1960s.

To see it now, even ignoring a roof that needs replacing and a foundation that needs rebuilding, it is hard to imagine lives were lived within its log walls. And that, said Eitsert, is reason enough to preserve these buildings.

"People can kind of see where they came from," she said. "Kids especially. My kids don't know what it's like to live in one of those things."

The Heritage Society has grand plans, such as using the village for authentic quilting and cider demonstrations. First, though, they must raise money—from grants, donations, quilt raffles and lemonade sales—to support the preservation that remains undone.

"It's going to take an awful lot of lemonade to take care of that building," Kathy Lund said of the McCann cabin.

And sweat. Winter belongs to the grant committee but come spring the work will begin again. At a Society meeting, a newcomer showed up who announced that he had restored three cabins of his own.

"We stood up and clapped and said, 'Yes!'" said Denny Lund.

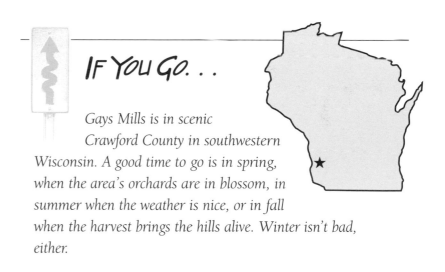

IF YOU GO. . .

Gays Mills is in scenic Crawford County in southwestern Wisconsin. A good time to go is in spring, when the area's orchards are in blossom, in summer when the weather is nice, or in fall when the harvest brings the hills alive. Winter isn't bad, either.

20
MOUNDS ARE HUMBLING, HISTORIC

HARPERS FERRY, IOWA

THE FIRST STAGE OF THE HIKE WAS HEART-HEALTHY AND THEN SOME, a huffing-puffing trek up steep switchbacks before the trail smoothed and flattened and the climb became a walk.

But the effort needed to reach the ancient treasures of Effigy Mounds National Monument was less work than investment, and the payoff was pleasure. This 1,550-acre park along the Mississippi River is an outdoor museum where mystery is the featured exhibit, all displayed on bluffs affording magnificent views in every direction—up and down the river for miles, back in time for centuries.

The park is about three miles north of Marquette, across the river from Prairie du Chien, Wisconsin. Established in 1949, the park is dedicated to the preservation of nearly 200 historic mounds, some dating to 450 B.C.

While other areas in the Midwest also contain mounds accessible for public view, the "Marching Bear" mounds in the south unit here comprise the largest known collection of effigy, or animal-shaped, mounds. The Great Bear Mound in the northern unit is most impressive, 137 feet long and 70 feet wide at the shoulder. Join such history with incredible scenery on a splendid late autumn day and, well, what's a little climb?

I began at the National Park Service Visitors' Center. Several mounds are located near the base of the bluffs, but the largest collection is found on top along Fire Point Trail. While it is a 3.5-mile hike, one way, to Hanging Rock, park maps also show shorter—but still most enjoyable—routes.

The walk itself is educational. Small signs on plants and trees tell of uses by Indian communities for food, medicine or clothing. Black walnuts supplied dark dyes, fiber from the basswood's inner bark offered cord for sewing and weaving, the long sharp thorns of the hawthorn were fashioned into fishhooks.

PHOTO COURTESY OF EFFIGY MOUNDS NATIONAL MONUMENT

No known use has been found for the American bladdernut, however. I'd guess it was the name that turned them off.

The valley of the Mississippi was used by prehistoric Indians for centuries, first by hunters of the great mammoth and other big game and later by the Woodland people.

Theirs was not the first culture that built mounds—the simple, cigar-shaped mounds here had existed much earlier—but the Woodland people were the first to build mounds in the shapes of animals. Mound building here ended about 1300.

Scientists have learned much from studying these mounds. Signs at Fire Point interpret how Hopewellian Indians scraped a burial pit for three adults—one a woman with arms folded—and a child, then covered them with earth and rocks to build the mound. Other burials followed, one on top of another, but whether all at once or over a long period of time isn't known.

In some respects what isn't known about these mounds and their builders is even more fascinating than what is.

Signs suggest that circular fireplaces often found in mounds "probably" were altars used in funeral rites, and that mounds shaped as animals and birds "probably" had mystical meanings associated with the self-identity of the builders.

But who knows? The mystery is much of the attraction. We know so much about so many things, but the most primitive people who came before us managed to keep something secret forever. It's nicely humbling to be reminded our lives are but a speck in time, however critical seems the crisis of the moment.

But this is a hike and not a philosophy lecture so let's move on.

Little Bear Mound has been outlined with pebbles to better display its shape. From there I followed Hanging Rock Trail to Great Bear Mound and a series of smaller mounds, and finally a side trail to Twin Views, which offered high sweeping gazes both up river and down.

It was calm and quiet, cold and windy but sunny enough to compensate. Below me was the big bridge connecting Wisconsin and Iowa (thankfully, the glitzy casino boat was not in sight) but upriver the scene was timeless. If a long canoe had suddenly slipped into sight I would not have been surprised. In season this is eagle-watching country, but I was entertained instead by a big hawk that circled and soared and flew so close it filled my binoculars until I didn't need them.

The climb, the investment, had paid off.

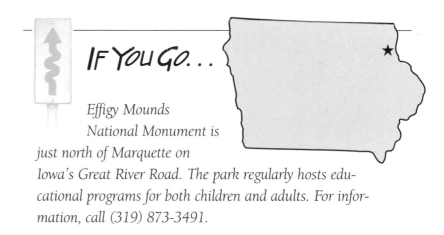

Effigy Mounds National Monument is just north of Marquette on Iowa's Great River Road. The park regularly hosts educational programs for both children and adults. For information, call (319) 873-3491.

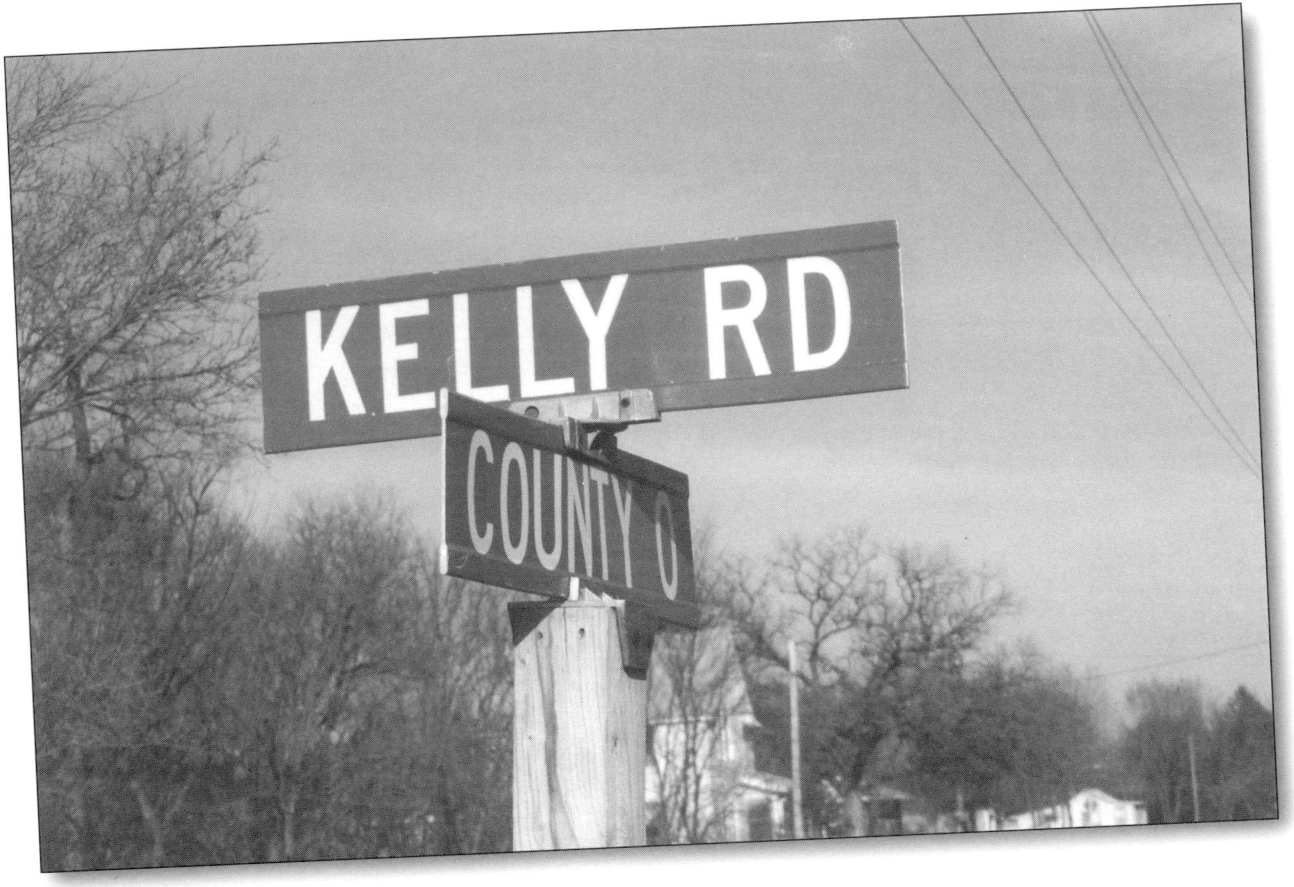
KELLY RD
COUNTY O

21
KELLY'S MISPLACED GRAVE

SHAMROCK, WISCONSIN

JUST OUTSIDE OF STOUGHTON, a small community not far from Madison, is an almost hidden little cemetery whose entombed population numbers a hundred or so Norwegian settlers and an Irishman. The Norwegians are spread over half a dozen hillside rows, but the Irishman is buried alone, only with mystery.

A small, gray headstone answers the who and when—Louis Kelly, 1839-1926—and the what and where don't really matter too much. But the why is a burial plot that has never been unraveled, at least not on any of the St. Patrick's Days I've thought about Louis Kelly since I trimmed around his grave while working a college job long ago.

Why? Why was Louis Kelly placed where he was? Why were the tired bones of a son of the sod spending eternity where only Norwegians were neighbors? And could a man of the green ever be happy on St. Patrick's own day if he observed it among lutefisk lovers?

Something suggests lefse and corned beef do not a sandwich make.

"Well b'gosh and b'gorrah, it's the great day. Let's rise and tip a wee pint for the blessed saint," Kelly must trill to his fellow reposers, to Gunder and Nels, to Knute and Lars and the seven ol' Oles lying nearby.

"Uffda," they must mutter in collective dismay. "This is Stoughton, not Killarney. Doesn't that silly Irishman know it's May 17 that counts around here?"

That day is Syttende Mai, Norway's constitution day and the biggest day of the year in little Stoughton.

Louis Kelly's grave situation came to mind recently when I passed through the tiny Jackson County community of Shamrock, south of Black River Falls. In the yard of a tidy country church on Kelly Road near Shamrock Creek, I came across the burial place that Louis Kelly was born to be dead in.

Louis, if you're listening up there, Shamrock would have fit you like linen fits an Irish lassie.

It wasn't always called Shamrock. Among its earlier settlers were Kellys, and the town's first name was Kelly's Corner. Even today, though Germans own the farms around it, there may be more Kelly girls—

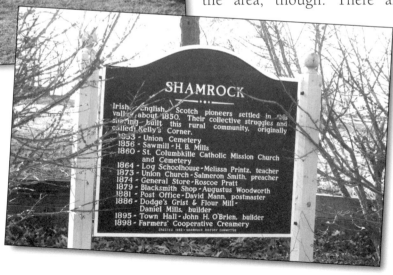

and boys—in Shamrock's graveyards than in any employment agency above ground.

Charles Kelly is to thank for that. He came from Ohio to the little valley that was to bear his name, with Margaret, the woman who was to bear his children. All 14 of them.

The Kelly clan spread out as its members grew up and married but enough stayed close so that Union Cemetery is still home to Oscar, Pliny, Elisa, James, Mary, Bernice, Carrie and Oliver, as well as Charles and Margaret—to name but a few.

Of course, the Irish being then what they still are today, the Protestants rest in one cemetery and Catholics in another; but Trudy Adams, who collected the story of Shamrock a few years ago, said the parties got along well in America.

The Irish did not own all of the area, though. There are

English and Scottish names among the gravestones, too, and there's even one Baptiste LaPoint. But Shamrock in the 1800s was mainly a place for the Irish, and the names in Catholic St. Columbkille's Cemetery surely would wet the eye of Bing Crosby or any old Irish priest.

The stones are hard to read but there appear to be Crossens and Doughertys from Donegal, O'Connors and O'Neils and O'Briens from O'Ireland, Susen Welsh from Derry and a lass by the name of Bridget Butler from Galway. Her marker is among the largest in St. Columbkille's and perhaps the most poignant, too, even 125 years after she earned it by dying. It reads:

> Far from thee Ireland, loving thee best
> Here have I come to find freedom and rest
> Home longing and all the poor exile can crave
> Are found in the calm, holy peace of the grave.

Well, Louis, your grave appears calm and peaceful and still neatly trimmed, and by now you've adjusted to Knute and Jens and the seven ol' Oles. Maybe you've even adjusted to lutefisk, too, though unless you went down and not up that probably wasn't a worry.

But without trying to spark an ethnic tiff here, it just seems somehow that you should have reserved a permanent place on Kelly Road in the hamlet of Shamrock, where the road would rise to meet you and the wind would ever be at your back.

It's too late for that now, though, so just rest on. And on St. Patrick's Day, top of the mornin' to you, Louis—and to all you Oles, too.

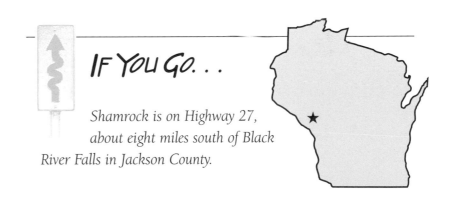

IF YOU GO...

Shamrock is on Highway 27, about eight miles south of Black River Falls in Jackson County.

22

BLACK HAWK'S HOME, AND LOST HOMELAND

ROCK ISLAND, ILLINOIS

THE SAD AND TRAGIC STORY OF THE FAMED, but ill-fated, Chief Black Hawk began here on flatland along the Rock River, a broad plain below forested bluffs where the Sauk and Mesquakie Indians long made their homes.

Other Indians had occupied this land since prehistoric times. Mounds, later destroyed, told that story. But the village known as Saukenuk was the home of the Sauk from as early as 1730. With their neighbors the Mesquakie, they farmed the land along the river and depended upon the fur trade for their livelihood. Saukenuk was the site of fighting during the War of 1812, and had been the westernmost battle site of the Revolutionary War; the Sauk made the mistake of siding with the British, which led Americans to destroy the village, at that time the largest single Indian village in the United States.

Eventually, they would destroy the tribe, as well. In the early 1800s Indian chiefs were tricked into signing treaties that would be disastrously harmful to their interests. In the early 1830s, as white pressure for more land grew, the Sauk and Mesquakie were forced west of the Mississippi River and, further, forced to promise not to return.

But Black Hawk, a warrior with more than 1,000 followers, did cross back into Illinois in 1832 in a hopeless campaign to regain their farmland. Their arrival threw the frontier into armed panic. Following several skirmishes that led to bloodshed, the Indians—many old, hungry and weary—fled north toward what would become the last significant Indian battle in Wisconsin. It would end in his people's massacre.

Black Hawk is gone but his homeland is now an Illinois State Historic Site, a 208-acre tract dedicated to his memory and the lives of the Indian people who preceded white arrival.

Central to that task is the Hauberg Indian Museum, located on the bluff where U.S. Army soldiers, supported by a volunteer company of men and boys called the Rock River Rangers, came with artillery in June 1831, at the outset of what is called the Black Hawk War.

John Hauberg was a Rock Island philanthropist with a passion for Indian history and culture. His interest led to the collection that forms the core of the museum's displays, including a metal-headed tomahawk and two smoking pipes that were believed to have belonged to Black Hawk himself. That is, while there is no paperwork to authenticate the claim, the items were given to Hauberg by Black Hawk's grandson, Logan.

"The family members came back here a lot," said Nancie Parkhurst, who conducts education efforts for the museum.

"Of course, they always considered this his home. The family kept coming back here because they had a physical and spiritual connection, but of course they got put eventually on a reservation in Oklahoma."

The small museum is housed in a grand lodge building constructed by the Civilian Conservation Corps in 1939. It includes dioramas with life-size figures depicting village life at Saukenuk, along with replicas of Sauk winter and summer houses.

From the bluffs at the back of the center visitors can gaze out over the Rock River countryside Black Hawk fought to save. "Sinissippi," as he called the river, "was a beautiful country. I loved it, my cornfields and the home of my people. I fought for them."

Now the land where his village was located includes a sprawling stone quarry, and where the Mesquakie village met his land stands a riverboat casino.

For many years the land that is now Black Hawk State Historic Site was an amusement park built by a railroad man to offer concerts, operas, vaudeville, amusement rides and other attractions. It had an eight-loop roller coaster and a Shoot the Chutes toboggan slide that carried riders down the bluff at speeds of up to 80 miles per hour. But in the 1920s the park was in decline and the state purchased the site for Black Hawk State Park, which was officially christened a historic site in 1987.

The park is great for hiking and bird-watching. Annual events include spring bird and wildflower walks, a September prairie program and a festival called Black Hawk Days, which honors Native American culture.

In the northwest corner of the site is a cemetery where many of the area's earliest settlers were buried. Black Hawk is not among them, however. He died in Iowa in 1838, a worn and broken man who had led 1,000 of his followers to death in a war that could never be won. He was buried sitting up inside a small mausoleum of logs. His grave was soon robbed, but his remains were recovered and placed in a museum.

The museum and its contents were destroyed by fire in 1855.

Postscript....

If you find Black Hawk's story intriguing, as I long have, follow his trail into Wisconsin to the site of his followers' sad undoing. Read on for that story.

IF YOU GO. . .

Black Hawk State Historic Site, which offers picnic facilities, but no camping, is open year-round. The Hauberg Museum is open daily except on Christmas, Thanksgiving and New Year's days. For information, call (309) 788-9536.

WISCONSIN
OFFICIAL MARKER

BATTLE OF
WISCONSIN HEIGHTS

On July 21, 1832, during a persistent rainstorm, the 65-year old Sac Indian leader, Black Hawk, led 60 of his Sac and Fox and Kickapoo warriors in a holding action against 700 United States militia at this location. The conflict, known as the *Battle of Wisconsin Heights*, was the turning point in the Black Hawk War. Here commanders General James D. Henry and Colonel Henry Dodge and their troops overtook Black Hawk and his followers after pursuing them for weeks over the marshy areas and rough terrain of south central Wisconsin. Yet because of Black Hawk's superb military strategy, the steady rain and nightfall, approximately 700 Indians, including children and the aged, escaped down or across the Wisconsin River about one mile west of here. Their success was short-lived. The war ended just 12 days later at the *Battle of Bad Axe* when many of Black Hawk's followers drowned or were slain in their attempt to cross the Mississippi River.

Erected 1998

23
GLORIOUS VIEW OF INGLORIOUS WAR

SAUK CITY, WISCONSIN

WE TRUDGED UP THE SNOWY HILL TO FIND THE BEST VANTAGE POINT, stopping where the wind blew cold and the land fell away to reveal the Wisconsin River, the Baraboo Hills and, even more distant, a tale still sad more than a century and a half later.

"From here back to the east," Wayne Schutte pointed, "is where the battle actually took place."

Wisconsin's last real Indian war, he meant.

Behind us was the mound where Black Hawk watched the tragic events unfold. Before us was a ravine—now cleared of brush and undergrowth and once again the oak savanna the beleaguered Indians saw—and the small rise where Black Hawk's fighting men had taken positions.

And over to the right, near an incongruous modern hay wagon, was where the pursuing militia's horse soldiers waited while other soldiers attacked on foot.

It was not a proud moment in Wisconsin history. On July 21, 1832, militia led by Henry L. Dodge and James D. Henry pursued Black Hawk's band of more than 1,000 weary and hungry Indians, many of them women and children, to this ridge, intent on eradicating the red nuisance in the way of white settlement.

That would be accomplished, not here but in a bloody massacre August 1 in Vernon County where the Bad Axe River meets the Mississippi, a place whites had the temerity to name Victory.

But the fight here, where grass grew as high as a man's head in the openings, was "the last actual battle where Black Hawk made a stand," Schutte said.

Now, everyone will be able to see where the Battle of Wisconsin Heights was fought.

Other states have battle sites where the public can relive history. Custer's dying ground is a popular park in Montana, and Civil War states have sites galore. The site of Black Hawk's battle became a public place in 1998 after two years of work coordinated by the Department of Natural Resources to begin to restore it to early 19th-century conditions.

"By doing that we'll be able to interpret the battle and tell the story of the Black Hawk War more appropriately," said Schutte, who is recreation coordinator for the Lower Wisconsin State Riverway. "To put the people right in the scene is what we're attempting to do here."

Battlefield restoration is a departure from DNR's usual mission. But Schutte and another DNR staffer with an interest in history, Dave Gjeston, were convinced the effort was the logical—even necessary—approach to the site, acquired by the state from a private owner in 1990.

"It's a cultural heritage, it's the Indian battle and it's the natural history," Schutte said of its importance.

Black Hawk's people were suffering when they arrived at this ridge.

They had left their tribal home near Rock Island, Illinois, in April, but any belief they could drive the white intruders away had swiftly disappeared. They were headed back to Illinois from Wisconsin when they came upon Illinois militiamen who drunkenly fired at, and killed, three warriors waving white flags.

There was no turning back then. Black Hawk's party went north again, raiding settlements for food, but General Henry Atkinson's men kept them on the run. It was July when

Dodge and Henry found their trail near Hustisford and trailed them through the Madison lakes area to this site.

"Black Hawk said himself in his autobiography, 'This is not where I would have chosen to fight,'" Schutte said, "but it was where he had to make a stand to allow his women and children time to cross the Wisconsin River. In late afternoon the battle broke out."

Estimates vary on how many Indians died; dozens, at least.

One white soldier died, a private named Thomas Jefferson Short, who was not short enough to disobey orders to keep his head down. Shot in the forehead, he is believed to be buried somewhere on the hill.

Black Hawk's band escaped in the night, crossing the river on rafts and other craft. But their flight would end in bloody rout at the Bad Axe, where hundreds were killed, captured or drowned. Again, a white flag had been ignored.

On August 27, Black Hawk would surrender at Fort Crawford, in Prairie du Chien.

Schutte said the Sac and Fox, as the Sauk and Mesquakie were later known, consented to restoring the site and offering public access. While most ignoble by modern reckoning, the events of 1832 were "not unexpected, not unusual and within the context of history at that time," he said, and interpre-

tive signs will reflect that. (In the early 1990s, the Wisconsin Legislature apologized for the state's involvement in the war.)

Volunteers have helped clean brush from large areas of the battle site but work will continue after the 70-acre site has opened for public tours. And signs will be posted to alert visitors to the significance of the battle.

The war preceded statehood by 16 years, Schutte said, but the timing was appropriate. The pace of development of Wisconsin picked up after the Indians were subdued.

"If this hadn't happened," he said, "Wisconsin wouldn't have developed the way it did."

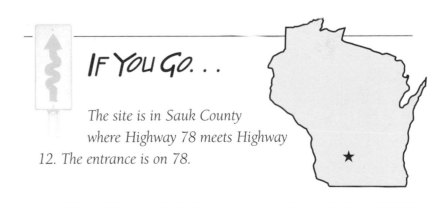

IF YOU GO...

The site is in Sauk County where Highway 78 meets Highway 12. The entrance is on 78.

24
STAND UP, BURN DOWN

NEW DIGGINGS, WISCONSIN

ONE DAY LONG AGO MOTHER LAROSE TOLD HER LITTLE SON, BRADLEY, the tale of the man who had been born 100 years too late.

"And she patted me on the shoulder and said, 'Bradley, you were born 100 years too late.'"

Mother knew best, of course, but even motherly wisdom can't force round pegs into modern life's square holes.

"You cannot escape yourself," is how Bradley LaRose puts it.

No matter. LaRose has found a way to live yesterday, running the tiny but treasure-filled Stand Up Bar and store in New Diggings, the one-time thriving mining town near the Illinois-Wisconsin state line, but he's still out of his time.

"This store's an anachronism," he says, stroking a glorious white-gray beard.

"There ain't no reason for it in a place like this. At one time, New Diggings was the third largest village in (Lafayette) County. (Now) this is the entire business district and it's just a place along the side of the road. This business is so small it wouldn't even register on the small-business register.

"But it works. I sell a few groceries, a little beer, give directions. Got a map published so people could find their way around. See, New Diggings was once the center and all roads led to it, but they're all crooked."

With 50 residents who call it home, New Diggings is far more alive than Natchez or Hardscrabble, other exotic but mostly forgotten names from the heyday of lead mining in southwestern Wisconsin.

But if it isn't a ghost town, New Diggings nonetheless is a sleepy little place, so sleepy that the day's first customer sometimes has to wake Fella, the dog, who then will "yike" to let LaRose know the business day has dawned. It dawned about 1:30 p.m. the day I stopped.

"Right now you might think that the whole county is out

doing things," LaRose says in half-hearted apology. "And other times there might be a dozen people stop in."

LaRose's store has operated in New Diggings almost from the earliest days of Wisconsin's statehood. George Watson operated the store for 40 years; his son, George, for 40 years after that; and then his daughter, Florence, for 40 years after that, until LaRose bought it about eight years ago.

From the front, it looks like any of us would feel after standing for nearly 130 years, a little weary, a little wobbly and a lot weathered.

But the view from the back best recalls the conditions in which New Diggers lived and sometimes prospered. The building has about nine additions, each one hung on the other like shingles.

"Every time the times got going good, they added on," LaRose says. "So kind of like Topsy, it grew, all the way from the 1840s to the 1890s."

LaRose's resume was built about the same way. Born in northern Wisconsin, he "was raised on a farm, worked in the woods, went in the Navy for a little while and ran a shoe repair and harness shop. (In 1980) I was looking for something and I didn't want to be where I was at before. So I remembered this and I looked Florence (Watson) up and I bought it."

LaRose buys, sells and trades antiques, the beauty of that being that he surrounds himself with the life he was meant to live anyway. Old guns, stuffed animals, mining tools, you-name-it—he buys, sells and trades. He keeps a few groceries on hand and more odds and ends than can be counted.

LaRose got a beer license for the store to supplement his income, and so the Stand Up Bar has become the social center as well as business center of New Diggings. Customers wear out one checkerboard a year, but that's the extent of live entertainment. There is a small wooden bar, only bottle beer, no glasses, no ferns and no stools, which, of course, led to the name.

"Oh, 'cause they were teasing me," LaRose says with a shrug. "Now you probably won't want to write this down, but if you have stools at a bar then a woman'll come in and put a purse as big as a suitcase on the stool and take up all the room."

Heck, put that down. No stools, no purses, no problem.

About all you can get besides beer or pop at the Stand Up Bar is fascinating conversation. LaRose calls himself a student of human nature and the immigrant history of Wisconsin, and his travels have yielded stories galore on both subjects: Irishmen he knew in the Navy, French explorers whose blood trickled down into his, Englishmen and Cornishmen, on and on.

What's more, most of his stories are true, too, unless LaRose tells you otherwise up front, though some of them he'll tell you not to write down.

"Oh, it's been an interesting life," he says. "And I might sound like I should be 140 years old. People say I should put all this down and make a book, but I'm not a good enough writer to make sense of it."

LaRose isn't too sure about writers, anyway. One time a guy wrote about his store and "he put in there that I was somewhat a distributor of bovine effluvia," says a stung LaRose.

"And he got that published! Now don't put that down, it's already been in there once."

All right, strike that part about the bovines.

Postscript....

Sadly, you can't check out the Stand Up Bar. In 1988 a fire turned the Stand Up Bar into a burned-down bar. A few years later, Bradley's son, Jake, built a new bar and store but that is now under new ownership and operates as Anton's General Store. But that is not to be confused with New Diggings General Store, which operates just across the street.

What the heck. Of course it's confusing, a town of 50 people with two general stores. In any case, New Diggings is worth a visit to see a historic Catholic church built by Father Samuel Mazzuchelli, a frontier priest now up for sainthood.

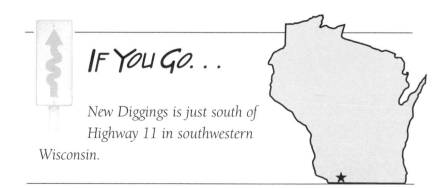

IF YOU GO. . .

New Diggings is just south of Highway 11 in southwestern Wisconsin.

25
CHAPEL IN THE PINES

ARENA, WISCONSIN

IT IS THE LITTLE CHAPEL THAT DOES MOTEL 6 ONE BETTER. The motel chain merely leaves the light on. Bill Akins leaves the light on and the door open, too. And the invitation is always the same.

Enter, weary pilgrim, and be refreshed. The door is open.

"There's no lock on it," he said. "Never will be."

They can't say that in the city. City churches have locks and keys and use them both and Akins understands why.

But here in the country, beneath a canopy of sheltering pines, a man can build a little chapel from logs and memories and furnish it with this and that from here and there and hang an invitation along Highway 14 for all to see. Since 1982, countless pilgrims have seen it and thousands have stopped to sit, to pray, to sign the book.

"Occasionally I have to watch that young people don't write dirty words in the book," Akins said. One local kid was mean enough once to scrawl lots of naughty things in the

book, but he was foolish enough to sign his name, which made it an easy sin to crack.

Most just write their names and say thanks, which is all Bill Akins seeks.

"It's been very rewarding," he said.

"We don't know what it might lead to by somebody just stopping by to see, you know. It might just lead them to change their ways," he said, but he makes no such demand.

"Up there, you can go and be there and be who you want to be. I ask for no donations."

Akins, 71, is a second-generation chapel builder. He was born in the Smoky Mountains of Tennessee, where nearly 60 years ago he remembers his father building a small church by a creek for the simple reason that people should have a place where they could sit and pray, or sit and think, or simply sit and catch their breath.

"Dad always said that anybody could have church services

tinkerer, too, and the memory of that chapel in the hills stayed with him through the decades until it could be reborn in rural Wisconsin. Akins finally started building in the summer of 1981.

But you do not build a chapel from a kit. For the logs, Akins cut pines that had been planted in 1942 by his wife's father, Ivan Ley, and hauled them with a neighbor's oxen to the chapel site on the hill.

The woodstove had once made heat for the Mounds Creek Methodist Church, so it seemed a good fit here. The windows—already 98 years old when he found them—came from a house in Mazomanie, the flagpole from the old Arena Union Free High School. And a UW-Madison journalism professor, of all people, donated a family Bible.

The bell—now there's a story. Akins used to work as a supervisor for Operation Fresh Start, which helps kids who

there as long as they preached the word of God," he said. "But the little church is gone now, and he is, too."

Akins and his wife came to Arena, an Iowa County village west of Madison near Spring Green, in 1948 and have lived in the same house ever since. He was a plumber by trade but a for various reasons wind up on the left side of right and wrong and need a boost back. When he left the program, the thanks they gave him was a bell to hang in the tower of his chapel and ring out welcome to all.

"The kids did it themselves," he said, "and of course I stood there and cried. They just weren't that kind, you know. I thought it was great."

He thought it even greater when another supervisor sidled up and whispered that the kids hadn't snitched it. They'd actually paid for it.

The chapel seats about 15 people, provided they all keep their arms in close. When we talked a few weeks ago, Akins was getting ready to get the small organ repaired. Some people who visited the chapel had left it open after playing music and mice got in and chewed it out of tune. That wouldn't do, not with the holiday season approaching.

Through the years, his little chapel has hosted 70 weddings and 19 baptisms and thousands of quiet visits by friends and strangers. But on Christmas Eve the chapel is his own family's special refuge. Some years ago, he built a small stable and fitted it with a crèche. He leaves it up all year, as if the other 11 months are all just a prelude to the last.

"It's very special here," he said. "Christmas, it means quite a bit. That's the birthday of the person who started it,

you know. Christmas Eve we have just a family service, more or less a candlelight service. We all take a part in it. We all have something to do, sing a song or some such."

His wife, their children, their grandchildren, they'll all be there in the chapel decorated once more for the holidays. When the night is dark and the stove is hot and the air is crackling like a fire with the nearness of Christmas, the family will gather in the little handcrafted Chapel in the Pines and be who they want to be.

Bill Akins asks for nothing more.

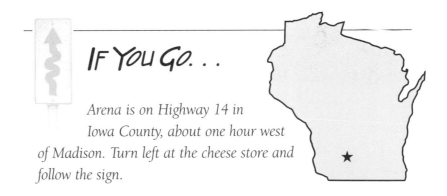

IF YOU GO...

Arena is on Highway 14 in Iowa County, about one hour west of Madison. Turn left at the cheese store and follow the sign.

26
RIVER COUNTRY BOUNTY

KICKAPOO VALLEY IN WISCONSIN

IN THOSE RARE MOMENTS OF SELF-DELUSION when I think I could live somewhere else I remember autumn in the hills, and know better.

One last look. High on a ridge, high on a crisp, bright fall day in lush-to-bursting southwest Wisconsin, I can see the quirky Kickapoo curling through the village, beyond the stores and the co-ops that serve the whole-grain crowd and the sprout people.

The famous orchards that have hugged the hillsides for a century are heavy with apples for pies and cider, and everywhere are the forested bluffs and valleys that were spared the crushing leveling of the last great glaciers.

On weekends, hungry hordes pour in from Wisconsin and foreign states like Iowa. But mid-week, when the world is working, you can find your own private Oktoberfest. Here is a farmers market as far as the eye can see, its bounty displayed up and down every country aisle.

And in the front seat and back seat of my car. Early in the morning, after breakfast in Spring Green, I stopped at Peck's roadside market to check out the horses made of melons and squash pulling a wagon driven by a pumpkin-headed teamster. The wagon is a tradition at Peck's. I always stop to see it and while there I bought a green squash and orange squash and striped squash and a very cool multicolored squash shaped like a turbaned head.

Garden art. If we don't eat it we can put it on the mantel.

It was the kind of savory day you would like to bottle and open in February. Along Highway 14 there were deer in the tree lines, cranes in the corn, turkeys in the hay. At Gotham (where I couldn't help but think a Bat Cave Bed and Breakfast would do well) I headed west on Highway 60, the curvy two-lane road that apes the path of the Wisconsin River.

The deer-crossing signs were pockmarked with bullet holes, the country equivalent of city graffiti. Outside Gotham, a road crew was building a new bridge across the Little Pine River, crawling over girders and smoothing wet cement. It will be nice for travelers, perhaps, but the work left some awful scars on the land.

I didn't stop at Muscoda, the mushroom city where in another season the morel of this story could be written. But I stopped to look at the effigy mound shaped like a bird in flight and to look for buffalo at the farms of the Ho-Chunk Nation on ancestral land recently restored to tribal ownership.

The buffalo were out of sight, but across the road a big old heavy-bagged Brown Swiss cow had just dropped a calf in the corner of a pasture, so I watched her lick her new delivery and collect herself.

If you think your HMO is stingy, consider this poor mother. By nightfall she would be back in the milking line. When one of the farm's owners passed by on a tractor I congratulated him on his new arrival—which surely must have confirmed his doubts about city folks—and got back on the road.

But not for long. The river wasn't hurrying, so why should I? The lower Wisconsin, sluggish and sandbarred, isn't like its hard-toiling northern self. There it makes paper and makes power; here it mostly makes peace with the land, drifting slowly as it nears the end of its long journey from Lac Vieux Desert near the Michigan border to the Mississippi. At Port Andrew, where the sun danced in shimmers on the river's surface, I sat on a picnic bench and skimmed the local papers, noting in the *Spring Green Home News* that the lower Wisconsin now has its own web site.

Will wonders never cease? The World Wide Web, and our river runs through it.

I headed north on Highway 131, back on mission, but decided Bell Center Road had a nice ring to it and went off to check it out. It was narrow, winding and lovely, canopied with trees in spots, then bursting into sunlight as it climbed the ridges. A man on a riding mower was giving the hilltop cemetery its last trim of the season and at the end of Dry Hollow Road was Bell Center itself, a quiet village with numbered streets, but only enough to get to Third.

Gays Mills was celebrating its 150th birthday in 1998. A store window noted the birthday event with a simple "Welcome Home Kickapoogians" but the community's focus was clearly on the abundant apple crop and the job of selling it to visitors.

Good thing, too. At Kickapoo Locker Services I bought bratwurst made with apple cider. At Kickapoo Orchards I bought a half-peck of McIntosh apples. And farther up Apple Alley at Sunrise Orchards I picked up caramel apples coated with nuts, and a bottle of cider.

Oh, and some cheese curds, too, because the route man stocking the cooler promised they were as fresh as curds could be.

How fresh were they? Yesterday they had mooed, today they squeaked so loud I could hear them over the car radio as I headed for home.

But not before the last lingering look that began this tale. High on a ridge, high on autumn, high now on apples and curds.

You don't need a tractor to help with the harvest.

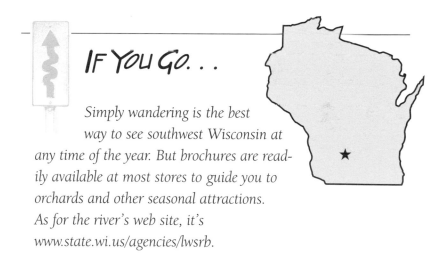

IF YOU GO...

Simply wandering is the best way to see southwest Wisconsin at any time of the year. But brochures are readily available at most stores to guide you to orchards and other seasonal attractions. As for the river's web site, it's www.state.wi.us/agencies/lwsrb.

27
A WALK ON LONG AGO LANE

MT. ZION, WISCONSIN

SOME ROADS BEG TO BE WALKED.

Not highways like 61 or 171; numbered roads were made to be driven.

But some roads demand slower attention because they ask the best question a road can ask: Where did that name come from?

I was on one numbered highway and headed for another in this hilly corner of Crawford County the other day when I came across a cluster of riddle roads that raised more questions than Bill Clinton's alibis.

Who was the child behind Childs Hollow Road? Or the bear behind Bear Cave Lane?

Why Sleepy Hollow Road, a steep drop past winter-shaggy horses, fattening steers and an "Old Man Xing" sign at the bottom?

Jeff's Drive and Jim's Drive even I could figure out, but was Hope Lane a dead end or a dream fulfilled? And was Happy Place Lane really that?

Wander and wonder, or you're wasting your time. Then walk. I parked my car and started off on Long Ago Lane.

It was one of those beautiful winter days that make you forget the bad ones. In every direction the sky was clear as a baby's conscience, a brilliant, buoyant blue. The February sun was a flashlight, not a furnace, but it did the best it could, casting artful shadows in the woods where it could not cast warmth. The wind was a breeze at best, enough to freshen the face but lacking the teeth to bite.

Long Ago Lane wound uphill. On one side pockets of trees covered a snowy hillside while on the other the roadway fell off into a little valley with a stream that wandered here and there. It was the stuff of postcards. Clean, fluffy snow from the night before still clung to trees and brush piles and lay thick on the flat stumps.

It was quieter than church, but for my footfall. In the trees

105

a branch snapped and a squirrel scolded, but while I cannot settle the eternal mystery of the tree that falls in an empty forest, this I can say: When a lone oak leaf flutters slowly to the forest floor, even if there is someone there to hear, it makes not a sound.

Long Ago Lane proved to be a short road but don't call it a dead end because that would suggest a waste of time. Up the hill and around the bend where it concluded sat two farms, one on each shoulder. One had a small red barn, now retired from dairying, and while a few hairy heifers chewed hay in the yard the pasture was empty but for animal tracks. They ran up one hill and down the other and up again, because this is country the great flattening glaciers missed so long ago.

Was that behind the name?

Wayne Mindham had not a clue, and he was my last, best bet. He has lived on the crest of Long Ago Lane for 30

COUNTRY ROAD PHOTO BY BOB RASHID

years, and when I stopped his truck to ask the inside skinny he only shrugged and smiled.

"This lady named it. She named all the roads around here and she's passed away," he said. "Mrs. Frank Devlin is the one that done it, but there's really no way to find out."

In 30 years, he said, I was the only one who ever stopped his truck and wondered.

Like a lot of country folks, Mindham doesn't farm much anymore, just the heifers and a couple acres of corn so the turkeys and deer on his property will have a place to feed and he will have wildlife to watch with the binoculars he keeps at the window. Sometimes eagles come up this way from the Wisconsin River and, of course, the hills offer the same beauty today they did when he moved here.

Mindham works in town now. There's less dairying in these parts than there used to be and more folks are moving in from other places to claim a piece of the country so "you don't hardly know your neighbors anymore."

But the essence of Long Ago Lane is still with us in the here and now.

"It's gorgeous out here, it really is," he said, his eyes sweeping the hills. "It's unbelievable, but we don't see it. We don't see it, really. You SEE it, of course, but..."

I knew what he meant. About that time Mindham's only neighbor came home and the three of us conspired to produce a little traffic jam on Long Ago Lane, if you can imagine that. So we parted ways, Mindham off toward Boscobel and me back to what I was doing, which was mostly nothing.

"Have a good day," he said as his truck pulled away.

I already had.

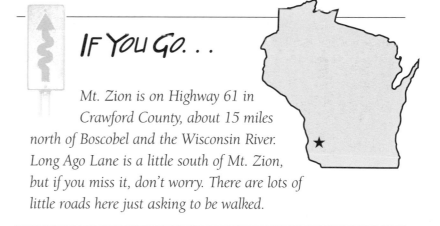

IF YOU GO. . .

Mt. Zion is on Highway 61 in Crawford County, about 15 miles north of Boscobel and the Wisconsin River. Long Ago Lane is a little south of Mt. Zion, but if you miss it, don't worry. There are lots of little roads here just asking to be walked.

28
BIG LAKE SPINS BIG YARNS

TWO HARBORS, MINNESOTA

THREE DAYS ON THE BULLY LAKE and not a shipwreck tale yet. Ahoy, then.

The winter of 1905 was a brutal one for Lake Superior shipping. Storms damaged 70 ships and claimed 78 lives, but no gale blew like the devil's own breath that sunk the *Madeira* just off Split Rock.

An ore carrier, 436 feet long and almost new, the *Madeira* was being towed by the steamship *William Edenborn* when horrific winds and blinding snow struck on November 28. The *Madeira* was cut from her tow, just before the *Edenborn* herself broke in half on the rocks, but she fared no better for her freedom.

She struck against a cliff so sheer and high the crew could not see the top. A line was cast but to no avail. The *Madeira* would back up and shoot against the cliff, over and over, "like an insane man trying to batter out his brains against a stone wall," one account put it later.

Amazingly, all but one crew member survived the lake and the blizzard on shore but the *Madeira* sunk off Split Rock, where a lighthouse was built a few years later of materials hoisted by rope and pulley up that same cliff.

Today, her anchor is on display at Madeira Gifts, which has a viewing tower out back where visitors can see the Split Rock Lighthouse, but only after passing shelves of souvenirs. The *Madeira* is dead; long live the sweatshirt.

That's my shipwreck story. And lest you think I overdramatized the weather here on Lake Superior's north shore, consider this: 78-year-old June Horgan won 10 gallons of ice cream for correctly predicting the day Two Harbors' last stubborn snow pile of 1997 finally melted away.

It was June 27.

Superior's north shore, where the land rises from the water into the Sawtooth Mountains, is a string of old villages with colorful pasts. Beaver Bay was the birthplace of the

Chippewa mail carrier John Beargrease, the famed sled-dog driver. Silver Bay was named for rocks along shore that looked like silver (but weren't) and a granite cross in Schroeder marks the spot where "the Snowshoe Priest," Father Frederic Baraga, found refuge from a terrible storm in 1846.

Long after the fishing and lumbering that gave them birth has mostly disappeared, Schroeder, Tofte and Lutsen are prospering again due to tourism.

The landscapes are stunning and, in addition to winter skiing, Lutsen now boasts Superior National Golf Course, a splendid layout in the foothills of the Sawtooth that demands shots over Poplar River rapids and even has a genuine bear's den—the ultimate hazard—next to the 16th tee. Fore—yikes!

After Lutsen, I passed quickly through Grand Marais and stopped at Grand Portage National Monument, a replica of Minnesota's earliest fur-trading settlement, but my target now was Canada. Customs was a breeze and, after stopping to trade a Ben Franklin for a handful of Queen Elizabeths (just don't expect this loyal son of Ireland to sing "God Save the Queen"), I entered the land of the voyageurs and Molson beer.

With 120,000 residents, Thunder Bay is the largest city on the circle tour and claims to be the world's largest freshwater port. And, like much of the Superior region, it owes everything to the beaver. It was Europe's insatiable demand for fur hats that brought French voyageurs to this part of North America and led first to trading posts and eventual settlement.

That era is celebrated at Old Fort William, a sprawling recreation of Thunder Bay's original North West Company trading post. Old Fort William is one of those places where the hired hands wear authentic costumes and, no matter how dumb a visitor's questions, answer in the language and spirit of 1815.

At the fort's entrance, I declined a voyageur's offer of corn in grease but elsewhere there were samples of gingerbread and historic food, and visitors and guides danced reels to the music of a fiddle in the Main Square.

About 24 kilometers (this is Canada, remember) west of Thunder Bay lies Kakabeka Falls Provincial Park, which my guidebook called the Niagara of the North.

It was magnificent, all right, the kind of must-see that makes Mr. Kodak a very rich man. After splitting at a towering rock upon which trees somehow grow, the Kaministiquia River falls 128 roaring, splashing feet and soaks shutterbugs on each side with its mist.

Four days on the lake now and no waterfall legends. Let's fix that.

It was here where Greenmantle, the tall, graceful and dark-eyed Ojibwa Indian princess, was carried by her Sioux captors so she could lead them in attack on her own village. But just as their canoes hit turbulent waters, Greenmantle swerved toward the bank and jumped to shore, whereupon

the surprised Sioux were carried over Kakabeka Falls and drowned.

Same story, second version. In this, Greenmantle died as well but her spirit lingers in the mist as a rainbow while the roar of the water is the warriors cursing their fate.

Happy endings are nice but there was a rainbow the day I visited the falls, so I'm going with the tragedy.

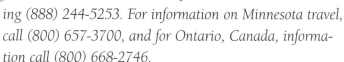

IF YOU GO...

The best source of information about Lake Superior travel is the Lake Superior Travel Guide *magazine, available for $6.95 from most area bookstores or by calling (888) 244-5253. For information on Minnesota travel, call (800) 657-3700, and for Ontario, Canada, information call (800) 668-2746.*

29
GANGSTER CALLED THE SHOTS

WINTER, WISCONSIN

I WAS STANDING ON THE FIRST TEE with my partner for the game, the ghost of the long-gone gangster Joe Saltis, thinking how the man who built this course might have answered the inevitable post-round query.

"What did I shoot?" he would reply, repeating the question for effect. "Boys, I shot a birdie, a few bogeys and, oh yeah, a nice buck in the trees near the 8th hole.

"No slice in that shot, boys. A hole in one!"

He had a blast here, Joe Saltis did. And if you think I make too much of the days when the most trusted iron in the bag was a .45, explain the "Lugerville" sign I passed on the way.

It is easy to see, in Winter in spring, why Chicago gangsters of the Roaring '20s were so drawn to northern Wisconsin.

For the same reasons the law-abiding were, obviously. When the heat was on at home, the north country offered cool lake breezes, solitude and recreational choices not available in the city. And for those hunted at home, it also helped that Eliott Ness was far from Sawyer County, where Al Capone built a lavish estate at Couderay and where, in the 1920s, a Joliet saloon-keeper and bootlegger named Joe "Polack Joe" Saltis built a lodge and golf course at Barker Lake.

One of his first guests, it is said, was Scarface himself.

By most accounts, Saltis was a fearsome competitor, in business or in golf. Newspapers of the day reportedly noted that those who crossed Saltis "went out feetfirst," and author Tom Hollatz wrote in *Gangster Holidays* that Saltis often resorted to primitive powers of persuasion. Primitive, but effective.

Saltis, known as the beer baron of Chicago's South Side in addition to his more impolitic ethnic handle, apparently came north when he tired of the Prohibition era's gangland wars.

He built the cedar-log lodge at the shore of Barker Lake—a wide spot in the Chippewa River—and added a tennis court, horseback riding, horseshoe pitching courts and rifle and pistol target ranges. For the nine-hole golf course, he imported rich black dirt from Tennessee.

No one in the area was much fooled by the new "resort owner." The boys who hung out at the lodge tended to carry weapons not associated with Northwoods hunting. One recent guest recalled the time a bear was sighted nearby, whereupon the "waiter" serving his dinner put down his tray, produced his gun from inside his shirt and went to handle the problem. But Saltis spent a lot of money in Sawyer County and that kind of green made friends out of skeptics.

The only real trouble he found grew out of his disrespect for legal details like hunting and fishing rules. He fished where he wanted, at least until the day a game warden named Ernie Swift slipped by Saltis' boys and arrested him at gunpoint for fishing too near the Winter Dam. Saltis paid a $50 fine.

Depending on which account you accept, Saltis either lost the resort over unpaid taxes or in a card game. Either way, it passed to other owners and has been operated as a lodge ever since.

Five years ago it was purchased by Tom and Sue Mike, a Hastings, Minnesota, couple who found out about the lodge's notorious lineage after they became interested in it, but who embraced the past in their marketing.

The Mikes have spent their off-seasons remodeling the lodge and updating rooms—there are nine nicely decorated lodge rooms, most with shared baths, and five lakeside cabins—and beginning to make improvements to the golf course.

It will never be mistaken for a championship facility but poses geographically distinctive challenges—think greens protected by trees—that make for some difficult shots. And any course located betwixt the Chequamegon National Forest and the shimmering waters of Barker Lake has something going for it.

"The place needed a lot of work," said Sue Mike, whose husband still works in Hastings during the off-season. "Some days it was, oh, what did we do? But it gets better each year."

They have already made friends of repeat guests, especially older guests who bring memories to pass. One recalled that his father had helped dynamite the woods to clear land for the course, and of course there was the story of the bear that interrupted dinner.

"You hear some of the old people saying that having Joe Saltis around here was kind of nice, because he spent a lot of money," Sue said. "I suppose at that time, with the banks (so unpopular) and everything, they probably treated the common people pretty well. They didn't cause any problems at all."

Fish near the Winter dam might not agree. But the day I

was there, they weren't talking.

Oh yes, what did I shoot? No birdies, unfortunately. But a few pars, a few bogeys and the better part of a workday afternoon. That's pretty good shooting in my book.

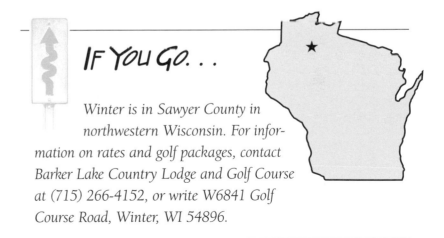

IF YOU GO...

Winter is in Sawyer County in northwestern Wisconsin. For information on rates and golf packages, contact Barker Lake Country Lodge and Golf Course at (715) 266-4152, or write W6841 Golf Course Road, Winter, WI 54896.

30
NOBLE HOUSE, NOBLE PURPOSE

FISH CREEK, WISCONSIN

SO MUCH SAWING, SO MUCH POUNDING.

New shops here and new shops there, new condos everywhere. Someday I half expect to find someone has ripped out those annoying little stone fences from a century ago (what is quaint when there's a dollar to be made?) to make room for Sold Our Souls Condominium Homes. You know they would sell.

Yet at one of the busiest corners in all of Door County, where Highway 42 falls down the steep hill into Fish Creek and bends right to follow the coastline (and, sadly, past the new development that blocks the familiar view of the park and creek), housing of quite another sort is under construction. Never mind that the building's namesake has been dead lo these many years; the Alexander Noble House, reopened recently as a public museum, has stood on that busy corner for over a century and it isn't going anywhere soon.

Imagine that—permanence in Door County.

It's nice to see that nobody thought to tear it down and throw up some condos, I said to Ellen Farrell, a summer curator.

"I can't say they didn't think of it," she said. "I'm sure there were developers who wanted (the corner) for shops."

But they didn't get it.

Noble was born in Scotland in 1829. He made his way to Canada and eventually to Door County, where he settled on Chambers Island in 1856 to work as a blacksmith. In 1862 he moved to the young community of Fish Creek, where he bought the property from town founder Asa Thorp for $260.

Noble wore many hats. He was a blacksmith and farmer, served as postmaster, was a town leader and served on the Door County Board. He was a man of some means, as evidenced by his family's 10-room house. He was something of a frontier renaissance man; he loved reading and learning and would gather his family around him on Sunday to pass on what he had learned.

The Noble House was not the first structure on the lot. Not long after his first wife died in 1873, his house burned to the ground. But his daughter, then 22, designed the new house and Noble oversaw its construction. The nails came from his own shop.

"I think this was kind of his therapy to say, 'We will build a new and better home,'" said Nancy Sargent, one of several members of the Gibraltar Historical Association whose families go back to Thorp himself.

After Noble's death, the house stayed in the family. Its last occupant was his granddaughter, Gertrude Howe, a pediatrician, pilot and something of a character, by Sargent's description. She lived in the house until 1990, when she entered a nursing home, and the house stood empty for some years while developers made quiet inquiries and members

of the historical group held their breath.

"It is one of the last houses in the community that has been on the same spot for over 100 years, so that in itself makes it of very historic value," said Sargent. "There was a lot of conjecture, and the fear was that a developer would come along and scoop it up because it was right in the center of town."

But after Howe's death, in 1995, the caretakers of her estate agreed the house and green space around it should be preserved. The Gibraltar Historical Association was able to raise about two-thirds of the cost of acquisition, and the town of Gibraltar came up with the rest.

Renovation of the house, now listed on the National

Register of Historic Places, began in 1996. It was in sad repair, in need of plasterwork, new heating, lighting and plumbing. Decades of wall coverings had to be replaced, wood floors needed to be sanded and volunteers never lacked for hard work.

But the house, which came with furnishings, clothing and papers and records that dated to Alexander Noble's day, was a museum-in-waiting. His blacksmithing tools were in the garage. The deed signed by Asa Thorp was found in his papers, along with a sketch his daughter used in designing the house. Letters to and from family members tell perhaps more important stories today than when they were written. Much remains to be sorted, dated and appraised.

"I think the interesting thing is," said Farrell, "all this information is in the house if we just get time to dig through it."

Few longtime residents or visitors miss the significance of preserving it, Sargent said, especially in light of the new development that forever blots out the view of Fish Creek's little park.

"We are perfect examples of witnessing that rampant change," she said. "That beautiful view that was all of ours is gone, and that really shocked people.

"Everyone feels, and this is a rightful feeling, that they have a little ownership in the house. I can call anyone in town and they just know what is going on in that house...and they're very excited about it."

On the day I visited, painters Mike Jacobson and Mark Bunda were scraping decades of old paint from wood siding, fully aware that their work would be judged by the house's fans. But that was all right.

"It's good to see there's no condo unit going in here," said Bunda, and Jacobson agreed.

"The only thing I'd rather see here," he said, "is somebody else scraping."

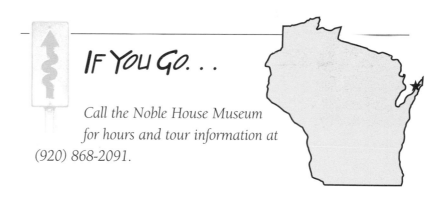

IF YOU GO...

Call the Noble House Museum for hours and tour information at (920) 868-2091.

31
A WALK AMONG THE STONES

MILWAUKEE, WISCONSIN

IT IS AS FINE A FORESTED REFUGE AS YOU COULD FIND IN THE NORTH, but it is here in the south, in the city.

But refuge it is by any measure, 200 acres of quiet beauty, with ponds and green spaces, little hills where you can sit and ponder the cosmic and the common and massive stone formations upon which the past has left its etchings. It is a Milwaukee landmark and a national historic site. And just as at the nicest state park on holiday weekends people are dying to get in.

Well, no. Not quite like that. This is Forest Home Cemetery, almost as old as Wisconsin itself, but in many ways less a boneyard than outdoor museum, sculpture garden and history walk all at once. It's 200 acres of Who Was Who. Park the car, I say, and enjoy it while you still can.

A respectable cemetery was one of the first orders of business for the new city of Milwaukee in the 1840s. Frontier burials would no longer do, so 72 acres of beautiful rolling land was purchased from members of St. Paul's Church and after a plank road was built to connect the city with its new cemetery the first burial took place in 1850. Eventually, death being an inevitability then as now, more land was needed and Forest Home grew ever larger. Today, if its more than 85,000 permanent residents were living, Forest Home would be one of Wisconsin's largest cities. Either way, they make it one of the most interesting.

Call the roll. Increase Lapham, early scientist, mapmaker and father of the United States Weather Service? Here.

Alexander Mitchell, noted banker and railroad enthusiast, not to mention father of the celebrated fly boy General Billy Mitchell? Here, and here.

Christopher Sholes, inventor of the typewriter? Here as well.

This being Milwaukee, food and drink are ably represented. Fred Pabst, the sea captain who married a brewer's daughter and stayed ashore to build the world's largest brewery, is buried at Forest Home, as are Valentine Blatz, who made the city's first bottled beer, and Joseph Schlitz, who made Milwaukee famous.

John Plankington, the onetime largest meat packer in the world, is buried here and so is the sausage king Fred Usinger, who got his start selling sausages to saloon keepers who offered free lunches to customers.

The big industrial names are here, of course. Edward Allis of Allis-Chalmers, William Davidson of Harley-Davidson, Henry Harnischfeger and Phillip Armour. Mathilde Anneke, the one-armed feminist who founded the first women's suffrage newspaper lies at Forest Home, as does Victor Berger, the first socialist elected to Congress. His politics cost him dearly in life—he was accused and convicted of treasonous thinking—but now he rests in peace.

There are enough generals in Forest Home to lead all the armies of the dead, at least a half dozen from the Civil War alone. Erastus B. Wolcott, the Civil War surgeon general, is one of them and so is Major General Charles Hamilton, the highest-ranking general in the park. James Cogswell, an admiral in the Spanish-American War, is here, and ably representing the enlisted side is one John O. Fairbairn, who couldn't really lose in the

Civil War. He fought on both sides.

The cemetery is one place where a politician can have the last word, or at least not hear what anyone else has to say. Henry Clay Payne's imposing stone describes the "sometime postmaster general of the United States" as "an able executive, a public-spirited citizen, a kindly neighbor, a loyal friend, a benefactor of the deserving," and who could argue otherwise? Whatever the historians might say, his marker says that Emanuel L. Philipp, thrice-elected governor of Wisconsin, was "a kind, generous, energetic, capable leader of men."

I like cemeteries for the little stories told, or merely suggested, by markers. The Pabst family, for all their riches, knew grief; one marker reads simply "Baby," for a child of Fred and Maria that lived but one day. Daughter Maria lived 10 days, Louisa three months, Clara Ann less than 14 months.

One Wm. Greenslade is remembered by a polished granite column broken off at the top, reflecting a good man gone too soon. A stone train engine marks the resting place of Max Schuster, while Howard Wolf's memorial is a carved stone ship just like the one on which he died at age 16. Alfred Lunt and Lynn Fontanne, the famous acting couple, are buried side by side, together in death as they were for 55 years of married life.

But Forest Home was for the unknown and the ordinary, too. In one corner there is a large memorial for all the victims of the terrible Newhall House fire in 1883, a tragedy that took the lives of hotel guests as well as a number of immigrant Irish girls who lived on the top floor. Foley and Finnegan, Flanagan and Fullmer, Monahan and Moynahan and Bridget O'Connell, too, they are remembered here.

If you come to Forest Home—willingly, I mean—be sure to visit the Hall of History where the stories of the famous are highlighted. But be sure, also, to walk among the stones and find the little stories. In Forest Home, oddly enough, history is alive.

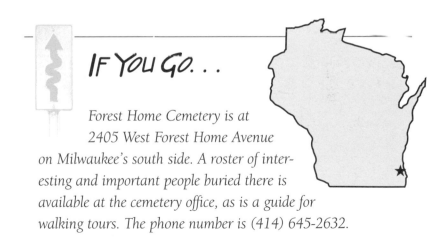

IF YOU GO...

Forest Home Cemetery is at 2405 West Forest Home Avenue on Milwaukee's south side. A roster of interesting and important people buried there is available at the cemetery office, as is a guide for walking tours. The phone number is (414) 645-2632.

32
END OF THE TRAIL

WAUPUN, WISCONSIN

LIKE COUNTLESS OTHERS BEFORE ME, I came into Waupun and found myself at the "End of the Trail."

Unlike the others, happily, I wasn't facing 30 to life.

One man's fate is another man's art.

You might think in a prison community that the statute of limitations would matter more than great statues of Indians on horseback or of Wisconsin's early settlers. But while it is possible to visit Waupun and not even notice the immense old hoosegow that houses the governor's many guests, it is not possible in this "City of Sculpture" to miss the legacy of Clarence Addison Shaler, whose story is one of umbrellas and punctured tires, a coincidental meeting with a master sculptor, and the nerve and talent to take it up himself—when he was nearly 70.

Shaler's is truly a Horatio Artist story. Born near Ripon in 1876, he made a tiny fortune through inventions, first designing a detachable umbrella cover while still just a boy living on his father's farm.

But Shaler's inventive genius was only beginning to reveal itself. Some years later, Shaler had one of the first automobiles in the state of Wisconsin when, fed up with punctured tires, he came up with a patch and vulcanizing repair kit that made him a multimillionaire. Inspiration is the mother of invention, but frustration is the old man.

The coincidence had come some years earlier. Never totally healthy, Shaler was in a Chicago physician's office seeking treatment for his ills when he saw a young man about his age laboring on a plaster figure in the next room. Curious, he introduced himself and the two men became friends for life. The sculptor was the later-to-be-world-famous Lorado Taft.

Shaler couldn't know that, of course. But from that day forward he also had an interest in art, especially in sculpture.

In 1923 he brought to Waupun a sculpture by Taft called "The Recording Angel," a figure of a woman with wings holding the Book of Life on her lap. The statue, which stands yet today in Forest Mount Cemetery at the grave of Shaler's wife of 26 years, Blanche Bancroft Shaler, took Taft two years to complete.

"End of the Trail" was brought to Waupun in 1929. The famous historical depiction of an Indian overlooking the Pacific Ocean when he reached, yes, the end of the trail, had been created by James E. Fraser, whose model of the image had earned him a $1,000 award at just age 20. The model for the work

was Chief John Big Tree, a Seneca who had appeared in Buffalo Bill's Wild West Show and who also was the model for the Indian Head Buffalo 5-cent piece.

In 1915 a reproduction of the early model won a gold medal at the San Francisco World's Fair, but Fraser did not have the money to reproduce the statue in permanent form, so it was disassembled. But Shaler, who had attended the fair, remembered Fraser's work and later commissioned the artist to produce it in bronze. In June 1929 the twice-life-size sculpture was installed near a dam on the Rock River in a spot selected by Shaler.

Shaler retired in 1928 and not long after that took up sculpting himself, working in a studio at his winter home in

Pasadena. In just over a decade he went on to produce numerous sculptures, including four that were placed in Waupun.

One of them is "Dawn of the Day," the approximate Indian translation for Waupun, which stands outside City Hall and grew out of Shaler's lifelong interest in, and appreciation for, the Indians he had observed as a boy. It depicts an Indian maiden casting aside her old deerskin garment, caught in the moment of change from her old native culture to the new one around her.

It represented, in Shaler's view, a new day of possibilities, and such was his attention to detail that the hands were fashioned after those of a nurse who had recently cared for him and the face was that of a girl he had met on the street in Pasadena.

Because he could find no girl whose feet were unaffected by wearing modern shoes, the girl's bare feet were modeled in part from a pencil study and from his mental image of an ideal foot.

Taft himself expressed delight in seeing the work.

"I cannot tell you," he wrote Shaler, "how surprised and pleased I am to see your charming work.

"How did you manage to outgrow at once the amateurish stage? Really, I am not flattering you when I say that the little bronze looks thoroughly professional. I have no criticism, only congratulation."

Shaler's other gifts to Waupun included "Doe and Fawn," "Who Sows Believes in God," and "The Pioneers," completed at the time of Waupun's centennial to express Shaler's appreciation for the state's founders.

Shaler also produced two works for Ripon, his hometown, including a statue of Abraham Lincoln for the town that was the birthplace of the Republican Party. But his second career as an artist ended in 1941 when Shaler grew dizzy while sunning himself at his Pasadena apartment and fell six stories to his death. Part of his fortune was left as scholarships for Waupun residents, gifts almost as lasting as his art.

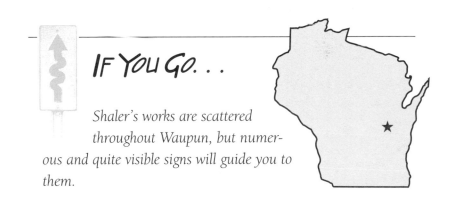

IF YOU GO...

Shaler's works are scattered throughout Waupun, but numerous and quite visible signs will guide you to them.

33
RENEWAL FILLS JANESVILLE GARDENS

JANESVILLE, WISCONSIN

SHH. THE BENCHES ARE TALKING.

Most benches just say, "come and sit a bit." The benches at Rotary Gardens are blooming orators.

"A garden is always quiet," says one bench along a flowered path, quoting Enid Haupt. "You never hear loud noises. There is a great, awesome respect for the beauty of nature there."

The lettering on another echoes Chief Dan George: "The beauty of the trees, the softness of the air, the fragrance of the grass and the life that never goes away. They speak to me and my heart soars."

And John Muir's truth is etched deep on yet another wooden resting place.

"When one tugs at a single thing in nature," Muir said, "he finds it attached to the rest of the world."

Nice. I wish I only could find a bench with words to describe the feeling I got when I first visited Rotary Gardens, a feeling approaching the exact opposite of déjà vu. I mean, I know I've been in this spot before—I learned to swim at the beach to the south and play golf at the course to the north—but I couldn't remember the place to save my life.

It's not that you can't go home again; it's that someone has moved around the furniture.

"It was a junkyard for awhile," said Robert Yahr, just helping.

Ah, yes. But junkyard no more, thanks to vision and volunteers. Today Rotary Gardens is a 15-acre botanical center reclaimed from a dumping ground simply because someone thought it could and should be done.

Again, a bench says it best. "We abuse land because we regard it as a commodity belonging to us," Aldo Leopold said. "When we see land as a community to which we belong, we may begin to use it with love and respect."

The vision came from Yahr, a retired doctor and active

and other groups the wasteland could be made to yield beautiful life. He wanted gardens like those he had seen in Europe, sprawling gardens with international themes, a visitors center for educational programs and blooms and trees the likes of which Janesville had never seen.

And that was how his garden grew. In May 1988 the land was leased to the Rotary Foundation at no charge. Contractors and volunteers hauled away tons of trash and hauled in 15,000 yards of topsoil to

Rotarian.

Early in 1988, while admiring what the local Kiwanis Club had done to turn a former gravel pit into a usable resource, Yahr noticed an adjacent lot where tires, empty barrels, street poles and other items had gone to die.

Clearly a man of no small imagination, Yahr decided that mere cleanup was not enough, that with the help of Rotary replace it. The first paths were put down, and in early 1989 the first trees were planted.

The gardens were coming alive, first the English Cottage Garden, the French/Italian Garden with fountain and formal pond, and eventually many more. The Japanese Garden, dedicated in 1992, includes a bridge built by volunteers who used curved light poles from the city's former wastewater treatment center to achieve a zig-zag effect. According to legend, people can manage the turns on the path but evil spirits, which can handle only straight lines, fall into the water and drown. The Sunken Garden is fronted by a great stone arch that once greeted visitors at the entrance of the Parker Pen Company's local headquarters.

Today there are 15 gardens, a restored brick building that serves as visitors center and education building. In 1991, 17,000 people visited Rotary Gardens. In 1997 the gardens had an estimated 70,000 visitors and hosted 60 weddings, all made possible because about 350 volunteers put in nearly 13,000 hours of work.

"I think they've done a great job for a community the size of Janesville," said Fox Point landscape artist Dennis Buettner, whose company did a master plan for the gardens.

The international theme "makes it very unique," he said. "It's important for a garden to develop its niche and stand out."

Buettner's company was rebuilding the North American Garden, part of Rotary Gardens' continued growth. Yahr envisions an arboretum eventually on nearby land that already serves the Ice Age Trail.

"In Europe, gardens take hundreds of years to develop, so I'm looking at it really long-term," he said. "This may not happen in another 10 or 20 years, but it's going to happen.

"Our slogan is, 'A community garden that's nice enough to show the world.'"

IF YOU GO...

There is no charge to visit Rotary Gardens. They are open for public viewing during daylight hours. Special events are held year-round. The gardens are on Janesville's east side, not far from I-90. For more information, call (608) 752-3885.

34
CZECH OUT THE NORMAN STORE

NORMAN, WISCONSIN

UNLIKE HIS SHRIVELED CORN AND WITHERED ALFAL-FA, then-dairy farmer Jerry Sinkula's future blossomed during the drought year of 1988.

Sitting on the lawn of St. Joseph Catholic Church during Bohemian Days on a too-sunny June Sunday, Jerry and his wife, Anne, were eyeing the old, empty and long-neglected house and store across the road, worrying for their crops and cows, thinking there must be a better way of making a living than waiting for stubborn rain.

The old store building was in a bad way, as weary and run-down as a sad man's dreams, but one thing could be said for it. It was for sale.

Only in the grip of drought would a run-down, abandoned general store and bat-riddled house look promising.

The Sinkulas made an offer far too low to be accepted, and of course it was. By the time rains returned and the grass grew green again, they were the uncertain owners of a needy dwelling and of an anachronistic general store that others had, years earlier, left by the roadside like so much litter.

Well, how you gonna keep them down on the farm after that? Wasn't Jerry a journeyman carpenter before he started farming? Most of us see a huge spreading tree and see only the leaves that must be raked. A carpenter sees furniture. The more Jerry stared at his demanding new house, the more he saw a bed and breakfast inn hinged on history, and so when he wasn't milking cows, he started swinging a hammer.

He's still swinging, but his family sold the farm and moved into the restored house in 1995. The bed and breakfast rooms were offered to guests in 1996, and shortly after that the historic Norman General Store opened once again.

All because it didn't rain.

Norman is little more than a crossroads on Highway G in Kewaunee County, about three miles west of Lake Michigan and six miles south of Kewaunee. If you get to Stangelville or

Tisch Mills, you've gone too far. Since the 1850s, this has been Czech country, and thanks to a renewed interest in heritage it still is today.

In 1856 a Czech immigrant named Simon Pelnar bought the land where the store and house now stand.

Pelnar's influence, and the land holdings of his sons, was such that the community was informally known as Pelnarsville until early this century. Some immigrants wanted to name their town Klatovy, for the area

of Bohemia they had recently left, but the postal service thought that name too hard to spell and assigned the more pedestrian Norman. Any complaints that such a name slighted Bohemians were wasted.

The structures that make up the Sinkulas' home and business are a mix-and-match set. The store building came from a site just west of its current home, and is about 20 years older than the 1904 house. The summer kitchen, on the other hand, has come home. It was built on its current site, moved to another community in the 1950s and brought back in 1992 to be restored.

The transition from farm to inn took time. Anne kept her

nursing job in Kewaunee while Jerry did part-time restoration until the farm was sold, which gave him more time to knock a century's wear and tear and neglect off their new old home.

There are two guest rooms inside, one with whirlpool tub but both otherwise furnished with family antiques, most with stories of their own. During my stay I slept in Jerry's Aunt Gusty's bed, for example. There were fresh cookies on a table in the corner and if I wanted milk with them I was advised to help myself from the kitchen.

The former summer kitchen in back is a two-bedroom unit with its own small kitchen.

The general store, once as much a fixture in small communities as the church and cheese factory, was operated by John Riha until his death in 1933. Later, the store was owned by other residents of the adjacent house. Then for many years it sat empty, a victim of improved roads and bigger stores in larger communities like Kewaunee.

Jerry might have had it restored and reopened earlier if he wasn't such a joiner. Since quitting farming he has been active with a state rural leadership program—which involved a learning trip to southeast Asia—and with Kewaunee County's growing agricultural tourism effort.

The Sinkulas were honored in 1998 as local residents of the year for their varied activities, but somehow the store managed to get put in shape for its second life.

It has a pot-bellied stove, of course, and a checkerboard for idlers to pass the time. The store sells camping supplies because a campground is across the road but the emphasis will be on Czech arts and crafts, imported Czech glassware, locally produced goods and produce and other items.

I say, Czech it out.

IF YOU GO...

For information, write
Norman General Store Bed and
Breakfast, E3296 County Highway G,
Kewaunee, WI 54216, call (920) 388-4580,
or e-mail at normanbb@itol.com. The store is
also a source of information for nearby ethnic attractions.

35
LEGACY OF PEOPLE AND PINES

BAILEYS HARBOR, WISCONSIN

IN THE PREFACE TO *Toft Point: A Legacy of People and Pines,* naturalist Roy Lukes envisions the impossible, "that absolutely every person, before entering The Point, be required to have read from cover to cover this book..."

This is not for the author's ego, but for his bottom line, which aptly for this special place is more spiritual than financial. Because beyond mere reading, Lukes further imagines "a written agreement swearing they will respect The Point in every way imaginable."

If the Ridges, where Lukes served as director from 1964 to 1990, can be held as a sanctuary, then the adjacent Toft Point Natural Area is a chapel in the pines. Something of a museum, too, reflecting the hard but rewarding lives of one family of early Door County settlers, that of Thomas and Juleyanne Toft and their seven children. But even more important, it preserves a forest of virgin trees and rare plants from the relentless push of development that so many mistake for progress.

A museum, in short, of one farsighted family's exceptional conservation ethic.

Those who enjoy Toft Point today, said Lukes, should be thankful for it.

And so I was after my first visit to the family's old homestead. It won't be the last.

The natural area, now under the management of the University of Wisconsin-Green Bay, covers about 740 acres on the point separating Baileys Harbor from Mud Bay, as the water was known when the Tofts arrived. The modern name for it is Moonlight Bay, but Emma Toft, the family member most associated with this place, always insisted that "Mud Bay was good enough for my people" and so should be for everyone else.

Thomas Toft came here in 1870, when shipping limestone from local quarries and timber from sprawling forests made the new harbor community prosperous. There was a hunger for building material in developing towns across the lake in Michigan, and huge quantities of timber products and surface limestone were shipped from Wisconsin's eastern shore.

Later, when supplies dwindled and industry faded, the Toft family operated a rustic summer resort at the point, without plumbing or electricity but always with Emma's excellent meals. Planked whitefish was a specialty, as were steamed cherry pudding, three-in-one sherbet and aebleskivers, or Danish apple fritters.

In more than 50 years, Toft Point Resort never advertised. Emma believed safe, quiet surroundings, beautiful shores and good food were enough to spread the word, and she continued to have visitors into the 1970s.

Electricity finally arrived. Yet as the world changed all around it, Toft Point remained as it always had been, safe from saws and man's heavy footprint.

Lukes can but speculate on Thomas Toft's insistence that his piece of forest remain pristine and uncut. Perhaps he saw the great northern forests falling all around him, or perhaps he saw the destruction of the terrible fires that swept through the north in 1871—causing the calamity at Peshtigo, for one. But something convinced him his old-growth pines should be left standing.

Juleyanne was the same with plants, having developed an awareness of, and love for, living things from a botanist who stayed at the point when the quarry was lively. Emma, who cared for her parents and their land with equal love and attention, once wrote that her mother "taught us to kill nothing."

When a spider invaded their rough living quarters it was captured live and carried outdoors. Flowers, in the view of

Emma's favorite sign, "are loveliest where they grow. Love them and enjoy them but leave them so."

From giant pines to tiny plants, the message was the same.

"Put your feet down as rarely as possible," Emma would say.

It was as if the family was honoring, in advance, Aldo Leopold's future plea for "the conservation of some tag-ends of wilderness" for those who would come later, Lukes wrote, that they might understand their cultural origins.

The Toft family did precisely that.

"Today," wrote Lukes, "this lakeshore forest is reputed to contain the largest continuous stand of old-growth white pine on the entire western shore of Lake Michigan."

Emma was also instrumental in preserving what is now the Ridges Sanctuary from becoming a trailer park. Lukes, as longtime director of the Ridges, learned much of the family's story from Emma, who died in 1982, 15 years after she sold the land at a bargain price to the Nature Conservancy.

The book was written to capture the history while people were still alive to tell it.

But further, Lukes said, "It's such a special place. The Toft family, in my estimation, was a couple of generations ahead in what they did in terms of preserving the point."

"Emma was just a great, great person. She was kind of in a category with Aldo Leopold...and people like that.

"I like the term role model. She was such a dedicated worker in everything she did. I truly feel that Emma could be looked upon as Wisconsin's first lady of conservation."

Today the narrow road that runs to Toft Point isn't easy to find. But visitors are welcome to hike, snowshoe or otherwise enjoy nature (except on snowmobiles and ATVs, obviously) as long as Emma's courtesy rules are honored.

Never litter. Don't smoke. Put your feet down as rarely as possible.

And please, don't pick the flowers.

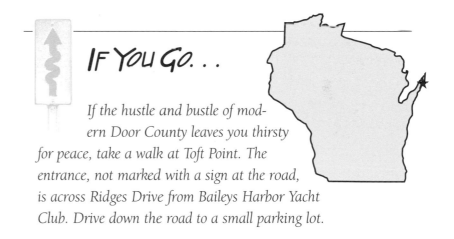

IF YOU GO. . .

If the hustle and bustle of modern Door County leaves you thirsty for peace, take a walk at Toft Point. The entrance, not marked with a sign at the road, is across Ridges Drive from Baileys Harbor Yacht Club. Drive down the road to a small parking lot.

36
LIFE REVOLVES AROUND OLD BARNS

ONTARIO, WISCONSIN

JOHN FISH KNOWS THE CYCLE AS WELL AS HE KNOWS THE SEASONS.

A dairy farmer all his life, Fish knows that the seasons come and go but dairy farmers like him mostly just go, a handful every day in Wisconsin.

Their idled, empty barns stay behind, though, left to wear, to weather, to sadly, silently, testify to what had been.

So on a golden day that was as perfect for picking corn as for merely poking around it was good to see Fish's barn not only in use but also on display. Fish was in the midst of what was turning out to be a grand corn harvest, and I was in the midst of what was already a grand tour of the many round barns in Vernon County, lured to his farm on a hilly Rustic Road near Wildcat Mountain by a guidebook I had received in the mail.

His was Barn 5, on Lower Ridge Road. From Barn 5, the book said, take County P to 24 Valley Road, go left to Rustic Road 56, left again and then right on Lower Ridge. And there it was.

Fish supposed if I wrote about his barn there would be more traffic on his quiet road to compete with harvesting equipment, but he further supposed that was all right. His wife, Gail Curry-Fish, was one of the guide's authors along with Wava G. Janey and June Zalewski, and beyond that he was rather proud of the old barn himself.

It was built in 1910—66 feet in diameter with a 40-foot silo in the center—and could have gone away like so many others if people hadn't cared. The roof blew off in a storm in the early 1940s, but a new roof was added and other improvements followed. Fish and his family have used the barn for dairying for 30 years, and during that time have added metal siding, a metal roof and a rectangular addition to house more cows.

"I won't say we restored it," Fish said from the seat of his tractor. "I say we preserved it."

So, good for him, and good for Vernon County because these barns are a treasure.

They say there are more round barns here in this hilly western Wisconsin county than in any county in the land, a boast formerly claimed by Fulton County, Indiana, until a visitor there informed them that Vernon County had more. But the claim needed documentation, so June Zalewski, then president of the local historical society, and her husband, Harry, spent weeks traveling back roads and byways, asking mail carriers, tavern owners and utility crews to point them to round barns.

They found 16, and eventually that led to *Round Barns of Vernon County, Wisconsin: A Circle Tour*. You expected, maybe, a square tour? I started in Viroqua, where a tile-sided round barn sits along a dusty street, and then headed off for the country.

Why Vernon County? In large measure the round barn heritage traces to Alga Shivers, an African-American who lived his entire life on a family farm (his father, Thomas, was the first in this area to purchase a tractor in 1917) in Vernon County.

Alga Shivers was born in 1889, attended college in Missouri, learned carpentry, served in World War I, returned to Vernon County and became a barn builder. He built a round barn on his farm and supervised the construction of 15 others in Monroe and Vernon counties, all of wood cut from farmers' wood-lots.

His step-granddaughter, interviewed later, recalled barn raisings where "Alga would get them started and the neighbors would come in and help. I remember Alga telling the amount of people that were there for meals; he always talked about what they had to eat."

Later, when innovations like square hay bales and mechanical milking systems left round barns out of favor, Shivers turned out conventional barns and other buildings.

Some of Shivers' barns are on the tour, along with structures by other builders. Of course, time has taken more of a toll on some than on others, but many have been updated and refurbished through the years and most are still in operation.

In truth, round structures aside for a moment, the circle tour was a barn lover's bonanza and the views of autumn approaching over the ridges only added to the adventure. There were structures of all sizes and shapes—tobacco sheds, dairy barns, barns that leaned like the tower in Pisa and some that had fallen away.

Regrettably, one of those was one of the 16 round barns, a structure west of Viroqua that blew down after the guide was prepared. But 15 remain, serving current owners in various ways but, just as important, representing the lives of those who were there earlier. The barn built by Alga Shivers for Joe Dank in 1921 is now owned by Dank's great-grandson, Gary, and a barn built in 1910 by Frank Lisker and his sons is still in the Lisker family.

But elsewhere the past is the present. On Pa's Road about eight miles east of Viroqua in Bloomingdale, an Amish family now uses a 13-sided barn that dates to 1913. Horse stalls and kerosene lanterns used by original owners are still in use today. In the first, nearby, two Amish men were loading corn-stalks onto flat wagons pulled by heavy horses, and if a picture had been snapped it would have been difficult to guess which of the last six or seven decades it represented.

Like John Fish, they have preserved a piece of the past.

Postscript...

After this column appeared in the paper, a reader wondered why I hadn't mentioned the old theory that round barns were invented so farm boys couldn't chase the neighbor girl into the corner. Now I have.

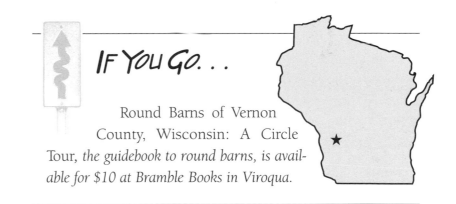

IF YOU GO. . .

Round Barns of Vernon County, Wisconsin: A Circle Tour, *the guidebook to round barns, is available for $10 at Bramble Books in Viroqua.*

37

HOLDING BACK THE WATERS OF TIME

FIFIELD, WISCONSIN

EVEN DAMS NEED FRIENDS.

Especially dams. And the old Round Lake logging dam, a worn and threatened relic of timber times long gone, was in desperate need when friends stepped in a few years ago to shore up its tired wooden bones.

Friends in need, indeed.

Once it was a key player in the great Wisconsin pinery that served as lumberyard for the emerging west. There were more than 100 such river harnesses then in Wisconsin's Chippewa Valley—a logger's paradise in the woods of no less than the timber baron Frederick Weyerhaeuser—but most disappeared in the bust that followed the boom. One survived, thanks to the friends of the Round Lake Logging Dam and the Forest Service. Now restored, its new role is telling stories. Not a bad life.

"People ask us, 'What was here that they needed the dam for?'" said Pat Schroeder, president of the Price County

Historical Society and a dam friend. The dam's job is "letting them know what a huge pinery area this was and how the dam held the river back...and how they got the logs set to go and how they got these logs to the river." How the north was won, if only temporarily.

The dam—called the state's last remaining structure of its type—is at the outlet of Round Lake along the south fork of the Flambeau River, midway between Fifield and Minocqua. It was built in the 1870s, when Round Lake was still largely wilderness area but about the time the incredible white pine stands of the Chippewa Valley were being eyed for exploitation. The region's many rivers and lakes offered easy transport for logs—as easy as moving huge pine logs could be—but dams were needed to give man sway over the rivers' flow.

Weyerhaeuser added the land around Round Lake to his empire in 1885. Logging took place in winter and, when spring melted the ice, the pine was shipped. Lumbermen lowered dam gates to build a head of water behind the dam, then released the powerful flow to float the pine toward the Chippewa and Mississippi Rivers and markets to the west.

Then the forests played out. Throughout the north, the depleted woods were largely abandoned, except for against-the-odds farming efforts, and by the early 1900s most logging dams were in sad repair. But the land adjacent to Round Lake was acquired by Otto Doering, a vice president of Sears Roebuck and Company, who brought a preservationist's sensibility. By the early 1920s he was making improvements in the dam's condition, even importing long timbers from the west because available supplies had been logged off, and he continued the effort through the years.

After his death in 1955, however, the dam was ignored. His sons sold the estate—dam included, along with almost 30 buildings on Doering's property—to the Forest Service, which was already administering nearby lands as part of the Chequamegon National Forest. The Forest Service sold the buildings rather than spend money to maintain them, but the dam and its moving parts continued to deteriorate. By the 1980s the dam needed restoration or to be put out of its misery.

Friends arrived in the nick of time. Formed in 1991, Friends of the Round Lake Logging Dam joined with the Forest Service and Price County Historical Society to raise money and interest in rebuilding the dam and to drum up a volunteer force to help with the work. During restoration the river was temporarily diverted while new timbers were placed on the original 19th-century base. Upright timbers were added and the center cribbing was rebuilt, using as much original material as possible. Construction was completed and the dam was rededicated.

But other work continues. Interpretive displays show visitors the history of the area and the role dams played in logging. A trail system has been developed—wildflowers change by the season and osprey and other wildlife are nearby—but other improvements are planned as time and money become available.

"This one is dear to the hearts of the community,"

Schroeder said. "Most of them, anyway, are thrilled to have it done.

"It's always been a fun fishing spot. Actually, it's always had a real aura to it. It's just become kind of a romanticized spot for people. There's just all kinds of things to see up there, winter or summer. We're really committed to it, to the point where we want to see it finished."

Considering it truly was almost finished, that's good.

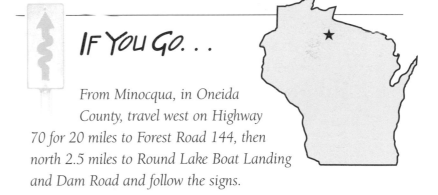

IF YOU GO...

From Minocqua, in Oneida County, travel west on Highway 70 for 20 miles to Forest Road 144, then north 2.5 miles to Round Lake Boat Landing and Dam Road and follow the signs.

JESSE JAMES

Northfield Bank Raider — This photo was from photos available at the time — 1876 — by Northfield Photographer Sumner to be used along with his souvenir series.

FRANK JAMES

Northfield Bank Raider — Photo was copied from those — 1876 — by Northfield photographer Sumner to be used with his souvenir series.

38

THE GREAT BANK ROBBERY

NORTHFIELD, MINNESOTA

EARLY IN SEPTEMBER 1876, while inspecting the new time lock on his vault, the president of the First National Bank tested employee Joseph Lee Heywood's attention to duty. "Now if robbers should come in here and order you to open this vault," the president said, "would you do it?"

And Heywood is said to have replied with a quiet smile, "I think not."

Less a hero, Joseph Lee Heywood might have lived long and prospered.

But on September 7, the 39-year-old acting cashier was true to his word, declining the gunpoint urging of a band of notorious bank robbers to open the vault. His noble concern for the money of others cost him his life. "Faithful Unto Death," it still says on a plaque placed in his honor on the old bank building, and each spring a planter of flowers is placed at his grave.

It's the least they can do. Standing up to the infamous James Gang might have been a lousy career move for Heywood—a couple of dead desperados and an unlucky bystander who bit lead that day might say the same—but it left Northfield with a dandy historical claim and a celebration for the ages. The site of Heywood's last stand is now a museum owned and operated by the Northfield Historical Society and the annual re-creation of the seven-minute attempted robbery and shoot-out is the centerpiece of a four-day festival that is one of Minnesota's best-attended events.

Yes, bank robbery has been very, very good to Northfield.

Jesse James T-shirts? You bet. But you don't have to buy souvenirs to enjoy the story.

There are some who still wonder if the gang of eight that rode into Northfield included the infamous Jesse James and his brother, Frank, semi-folk heroes thanks to the dime novels of the day, but really just robbers and killers at heart. Minnesota was well north of the bank-robbing brothers'

Missouri comfort zone, but evidence then, and research later, suggested they were indeed in the saddle that day.

Jesse's own biographer accepts it. Jesse died with a bullet in his leg that historians have traced to the Northfield shoot-'em-up.

There is no doubt about the others— Cole Younger and his brothers, James and

Robert, Clel Miller, Bill Stiles and Charlie Pitts. They had roamed around in Minnesota for several days before they settled on the First National as their target, and in groups of two and three they arrived in Northfield in time to have a nice meal before undertaking their gunpoint withdrawal.

Unfortunately the meal included whisky for some, which Cole Younger later blamed for what went wrong. According to the official account, three men entered the bank while the others stood watch outside, but while Heywood was inside refusing entry to the vault a hardware merchant outside the bank sniffed out the gang's intentions and sounded the alarm.

"Get your guns, boys. They are robbing the bank!" he hollered, and so Northfield citizens grabbed whatever arms were handy and opened fire. In the chaos that ensued Stiles, Miller and a poor immigrant Swede who hadn't understood the orders

Joseph Lee Heywood

to run and hide were shot dead in the street. Hearing the deadly commotion the robbers inside the bank ran out, but not before one—thought to be Frank James—shot the stubborn Heywood in the head.

Visitors to Northfield today can view some of the pistols used in the gunfight, a saddle that belonged to one of the bandits, the spurs of Bill Stiles and a pipe inscribed with the name "Tom Howard," which was Jesse's alias. There is a short video describing the attempted heist and the furious chase that followed. While Jesse and Frank escaped to Missouri, a posse eventually caught up with the rest of the gang and those who survived that shoot-out were sent to Stillwater State Prison. A couple of inlaid boxes made by the Younger brothers at Stillwater are also on display.

Jesse died six years later, shot in the back by "the coward" Bob Ford. Frank went to prison but was later exonerated of his crimes by a sympathetic legislature and went on to preach against crime.

It's all described in the museum. And if that isn't enough larcenous fun visitors can also drive the "Outlaw Trail," which includes stops at Oddfellows Grove, where the gang gathered that fateful day, Heywood's former residence, the site of the tavern where Frank James and Bob Younger were said to have overfortified themselves with bracing spirits and various sig-

nificant points along their escape route.

But for me, the best part was the now restored bank interior and the vault that Joseph Lee Heywood defended to his death.

The funny thing was, if the robbers had simply grabbed the handle and pulled on the closed door, so much bloodshed might have been avoided.

It wasn't, as it turned out, locked at all.

IF YOU GO. . .

Northfield, also the home of St. Olaf College and Carleton College, is about 35 miles south of Minneapolis and St. Paul. The Defeat of Jesse James Days, said to be one of the largest annual all-volunteer celebrations in Minnesota, is held on the weekend after Labor Day. For information, call the Northfield Convention and Visitors Bureau at (800) 658-2548, or visit them at www.northfieldchamber.com.

39
A WINDOW TO THE MARSH

HORICON MARSH IN WISCONSIN

THE HORICON MARSH IS ABOUT BIRDS, OF COURSE.

It's 31,000 acres of ducks, geese and maybe, if you walk the trails to Scaup Pool at the right time, a swan or two, like the pair of shiny white trumpeters idling in the pond one day last week. Rare birds, rare sights.

Sights and sounds. When the great flocks arrive, the marsh is a concert hall for autumn's cacophonous symphony, the harmony of the honk section punctuated by shotgun blasts.

And on the morning I came to take a walk, the marsh was a canvas for nature's weary expression, all rusted gold foliage set against a sky of baby blue. Once a skein of Canada geese crossed in front of the long, thin plume of a distant jet, the oldest flight of all transposed against the new.

But the great marsh is about so much more—about glaciers and evolution and change, about centuries of Indian culture that preceded the arrival of white Europeans who thought they could tame it with dams and dreams, both eventually abandoned.

So much of that is largely invisible now. Today there is no evidence of the onetime Lake Horicon, the largest man-made lake in the world where steamboats carried passengers and freight, though still buried in the undergrowth are the old stone fences that tell of later generations' failed efforts to make a marsh into productive farms. It was to tell these hidden stories that the Marsh Haven Nature Center was born.

The center that now covers 47 acres just east of Waupun was conceived around Larry Vine's kitchen table in 1984.

A wildlife research technician with the State Department of Natural Resources, Vine proposed to a small group of bird enthusiasts the establishment of a center to provide students and others with nature education.

Sure, thousands of visitors flocked to the Horicon each year to watch the bird migration, he said, but so little of the full story was available then.

"The more I learned about the marsh history and wildlife, the more I saw there was a real need (for it)," Vine said.

That idea and, as Vine always says, five cents of funding put the center into motion. A few small contributions came in, then a few more; volunteers joined the effort. But development of the center, Vine said, moved at the speed of money.

"If it didn't come in, we just waited."

And worked. Nature trails were established first, both through woodlands and over wetlands. While that project was under way, a woman named Barbara Gould stopped at the fledgling center, picked up a brochure and, Vine said, "caught the sense that we were trying to do something important here."

Gould's father, Lee, had just died. He was a true outdoorsman who had loved the Horicon Marsh, and she was looking for a suitable memorial. It came in the form of an observation deck along the Woodlands Trail, a 30-foot tower with a grand overview of the marsh. The tower was designed by an architect who volunteered his services and built by others who offered time and material.

"It taught me the real power of volunteers and working cooperatively," Vine said. "From there we went on (but) I would say that tower really put us on the map."

In the next few years Marsh Haven volunteers added a picnic shelter and bunkhouse for visiting school groups, scouts and others and, finally, the center's main building.

In recent years, the center's exhibit space has been expanded to include displays on wetlands and wildlife, American Indian life, the story of early pioneers and other stories about Horicon Marsh. An apartment for student naturalists was provided to allow the center to attract qualified interns. There is also a room—the Respect Our Earth Theater—where slide shows and other nature programs can be offered.

Today an active corps of about 30 volunteers, part of a supporting membership of 750 or so, works to keep the doors open for an estimated 25,000 visitors a year. On weekends, Vine and his wife, Sandy, are usually on hand, along with Vine's three-foot corn snake, also a volunteer.

"He's quite an asset to our center," Vine said. "It's an excellent conversation starter. It sure gets people's attention."

I'm sure it does, and that's fine, as startled as some might be. An "eeek" is as much a part of nature as a honk.

IF YOU GO. . .

The Marsh Haven Nature Center is closed during the coldest part of winter but open to the public seven days a week May 15 through November, and perhaps into December if fall runs late. The center is on Highway 49, three miles east of Waupun. For information, call (920) 324-5818.

40
A LIGHT IN THE NIGHT

BIG BAY, MICHIGAN

ONE NIGHT ON THE SOUTHERN EDGE OF THE GREAT-EST GREAT LAKE I sat in the crow's nest of a lighthouse and watched the sky, moody and mottled where it wasn't dark with anger.

It was raining, as it had been through the day, and the forest around me in the last light of evening was deep green beyond belief. Superior's waves rolled in and back, hypnotic and restful, and as darkness grabbed the night the beacon near my head began to blink, honoring the centuries-old promise of men on land to those at sea. Once, then again, the first blinks of another night of protecting Lake Superior's sailors from her legendary wrath, not that her mood this night was much more than a summertime snit.

But watchful I was, 120 feet above the rain-dotted lake, because the price of admission at Big Bay Lighthouse Bed and Breakfast gets you a bed and breakfast and a button that makes every guest an assistant keeper for the day.

It is not an amenity to be taken lightly. It was life-or-death duty, I told myself as I climbed into the tower, and Gordon Lightfoot would get no sequel this night, not with Dennis McCann, assistant—yawn—keeper on the job.

It seemed a fitting place to rest and take stock of a week of roaming Superior's shore, the last leg of which had begun in the fog of Sault Ste. Marie, Ontario, where I had crossed the big bridge to America and then headed west through Michigan's Upper Peninsula.

Get this—it was even raining when I reached Paradise, which didn't seem right at all. Rain and fog conspired to cancel my planned visit to the dunes and waterfalls of Pictured Rocks National Lakeshore, though conditions eased enough to permit a personal inspection of the popular Tahquamenon Falls, where I was delighted to overhear a woman tell her grumpy husband, "You can wait for us in the brewpub."

Brewpub? In a state park? Had Yogi and the Hamm's bear

created the ultimate merger? It was true. A brewpub had opened at the park's visitor center, which at least allowed me on this rainy day to find new meaning in "let it pour." But not for long, because a dry bed awaited in the lonely lighthouse at the end of a wooded lane near Big Bay.

The lighthouse, one of the few residential lighthouses on the Great Lakes, was commissioned in 1892 after numerous shipwrecks had argued for its existence, and began service in 1896.

Lighting the night might seem simple enough duty but however much we romanticize it, lighthouse life was difficult. Drinking water had to be hauled from the lake in buckets and lone-

PHOTO COURTESY OF BIG BAY POINT LIGHTHOUSE

liness and deprivation made it hard to attract good keepers. The first keeper, William Prior, went through any number of ill-fitting helpers, including one whose wife didn't want him working so hard and another whose claimed bad back only eased on weekends when he was off.

Finally, Prior's son got the job, but he soon fell and suffered what would be fatal injuries. Prior was so despondent that after he returned from burying his son in Marquette he disappeared with his gun and some strychnine. The "Help Wanted" sign went out again.

One other death has helped make Big Bay famous.

In the 1950s, after the light had been automated, the Coast Guard leased the facility to the army to train antiaircraft artillery. Planes would tow targets over the lake while soldiers on the bluff would blast away.

One of the soldiers, jealous because he suspected the intentions of the man who owned the nearby Lumberjack Tavern toward the soldier's wife, killed the tavern keeper. That became the basis for the book *Anatomy of a Murder*, and parts of the famous movie that followed were filmed here at the Thunder Bay Inn, a former vacation retreat for Henry Ford and today a public inn. The movie featured Jimmy Stewart, Lee Remick and George C. Scott, whose pictures hang on the walls of the inn, and by great coincidence I noticed during dinner that Stewart's face was on the television above the bar as well.

He had died that very day.

A small world? I thought of that while I sat alone in the lighthouse tower, posing as keeper on a dark and stormy night. Alone with the memory of Jimmy Stewart. Alone with the memory of poor pressured Prior. And alone with all the ships at sea, wherever they were in the inky night.

IF YOU GO...

For information on Big Bay Lighthouse Bed and Breakfast, call (906) 345-9957, or write PO Box 3, Big Bay, MI 49808. Its web site is www.lighthousebandb.com. A handy guide to Big Bay and other communities on Lake Superior is the Lake Superior Travel Guide magazine, which includes a detailed map of the circle tour, information on cities and attractions and suggestions on where to stay and dine. It can be ordered by calling (888) 244-5253.

41
THE OLD WAY HOME

TREMPEALEAU, WISCONSIN

THE MORNING INTERVIEW HAD BEGUN LATE AND RUN LONG, and afternoon had come early. I was behind schedule and, worse, behind a slowpoke when what I wanted to be was heading home, hell-bent for hurrying.

Then I came upon the Historic Trempealeau Hotel, which has been sitting in one place staring at the Mississippi River for 125 years. I was embarrassed to be in such a hurry, so I stopped for a burger and a beer and a good long gaze at the great wet way and left a changed man, now of a mind to skip the Interstate and take the old way home.

Interstates are for truckers and salesfolk and those who simply must get from here to there in a hurry, but the old way—longer, slower, hillier, more meandering—is for riding. I recommend it.

The old way home for me is Highway 14 through western Wisconsin's Coulee Country. Ole and Lena country, too, because even today in Coon Valley and Westby, you can't miss the evidence that Vernon County's roots were planted firmly in lutefisk. Westby was named for one Ole Westby, and the first settler in Coon Valley was Helge Gulbrandson. For a time, the village was called Helgedalen, for Helge Valley, until the name was changed to reflect the large number of raccoons in the area.

Even today, the little towns are so Norwegian you expect to find a fjord dealer on the corner. Westby has had a Norwegian bakery since 1905 and the Uff-da-Mart bills itself as the biggest little store in town. A sign outside the meat market even boasted 1997 Grand Champion Bologna, which impressed me no end. I would have expected to find that outside the State Capitol.

Coulee Country was itself in prizewinning form, its hillsides covered with contoured strips of tall corn and newly-shorn hay, the farm version of Mohawk haircuts. Tobacco plants in small plots up and down the road were broad and leafy, but the open-shuttered sheds where the crop will soon be hung to dry were old and worn, suggesting a crop with more past than future.

Viroqua, happily, looked like a town with both past and future. Its old Main Street had a nicely refurbished look, but the downtown had not gone so uptown that an Amish couple looked out of place while doing their shopping.

Even better, the marquee lights were on at the Temple Theater. The building is in the middle stages of rebirth—

those things take time in small towns—but enough restoration had been completed to throw a benefit concert that very night to raise money for heating and air-conditioning. I learned later that a full house came to hear native son Bob Hirsch play jazz piano, and what town of any size wouldn't want a full house on Main Street on a weeknight?

From Viroqua the highway climbed another hill and made for Readstown and Kickapoo country. I crossed the muddy little river, decided against stopping at Crazy Frank's cheap-as-peanuts liquidation superstore and kept on through Bosstown, where someone had posted a hand-scrawled "Beware of Lost Cat" sign. Unless they meant the missing lynx, it seemed like overkill, but I kept my eyes open for the few seconds it took to get out of town.

Legend has it the town was named for a mill owner who was so tough on his family he became known as Boss. Today, the place is so deserted someone has posted those black shadow cowboy cutouts to wave at passersby. Faux neighborliness, I guess. But I kept on, skirting Boaz, not even stopping for Richland Center, pausing only to admire the sign for Henpeck Road just outside Gotham. I would love to know the story behind that name, and would bet the rent it had nothing to do with chickens.

Vegetable season was in full swing near Spring Green, those glorious days of tender corn and juicy tomatoes. It might be just my imagination, but farmers more often park their pretty daughters in pickup trucks to sell corn by the dozen than they do their gangly sons, or maybe that's just good marketing. I crossed the Wisconsin River, passed Tower Hill State Park where my camping career ended with full surrender to mosquitoes 15 years ago and, for a change, even went right through Arena without stopping for curds.

Mazomanie, which came from an Indian word for "iron that walks," is finding new tourist life in trains that don't even come to town these days. History is the hook now, both in preservation of significant buildings and in heritage tourism. Mazo is the (sometimes unwilling) sister city of Black Earth, named for obvious reasons but now famous for having one of the largest shore stores in creation. Nearby Cross Plains, on the other hand, is famous for the designated "Gopher Crossing" in front of a downtown tavern and I vow that some day I will stop to ask what that was all about.

But not today. It was near the outskirts of Madison that I realized I hadn't taken the old way home in a long time because I didn't live in Madison any more. Needing to finally get from here to there, I joined the truckers and the salesfolk on the freeway to Milwaukee, later than planned but with only one regret.

It wasn't Henpeck Road.

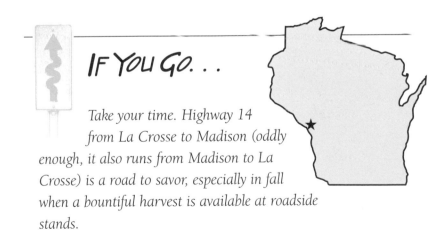

IF YOU GO...

Take your time. Highway 14 from La Crosse to Madison (oddly enough, it also runs from Madison to La Crosse) is a road to savor, especially in fall when a bountiful harvest is available at roadside stands.

I hope you enjoyed the ride.
Thank you for coming along.

People often ask how I find the places I write about and the short answer is that there
is no short answer. Some places—Galena and Door County, for example—
are well known but always good for new explorations.
Even the familiar can suddenly strike your fancy in a new way.

Other times, like the apostle Paul getting knocked from his ass on a dusty road,
I'm struck by something completely unexpected while on the way to somewhere else.
I didn't leave home intending to discover Long Ago Lane, but I was glad I did.
And I was on my way to a library when mysteries in a small town cemetery
seemed more interesting.

Occasionally I'll read or hear about a new place worth investigating, but the best
recommendations often come from readers. If you know of a place I should include in
my travels, send me a note at the Milwaukee Journal Sentinel, Box 661,
Milwaukee, WI 53211, or e-mail me at dmccann@onwis.com.

Come on, this is your chance. Tell me where to go.

— DENNIS MCCANN

To order
Dennis McCann
TAKES YOU FOR A RIDE

or for a free catalog of Amherst Press *Books-To-Go* titles,
call 1-800-333-8122 or
visit our web site: http://www.AmherstPress.com.

Amherst Press
a division of Palmer Publications, Inc.

PO Box 296
Amherst, WI 54406